It Wasn't Just a Job;
It Was an Adventure

3/28/2003

To Elizabeth,
  Thank you for being a friend
and a fellow conservative.
Enjoy reading.

Don Johnson

It Wasn't Just a Job;
It Was an Adventure

SAILOR STORIES

from U.S. Navy Sailors
of WWII, Vietnam, Persian Gulf
and Peacetime Deployments

Donald Johnson

Writers Club Press
New York   Lincoln   Shanghai

It Wasn't Just a Job; It Was an Adventure
SAILOR STORIES from U.S. Navy Sailors of WWII, Vietnam,
Persian Gulf and Peacetime Deployments

Writers Club Press
an imprint of iUniverse, Inc.

For information address:
iUniverse
2021 Pine Lake Road, Suite 100
Lincoln, NE 68512
www.iuniverse.com

We acknowledge the following publishers and individuals for permission to
reprint the following material. (Note: The stories, testimonials, devotionals
and poems that were penned anonymously or that were written by Don
Johnson, LT, USN (Ret), ex-RM1 are not included in this listing.)

ISBN: 0-595-26102-7 (Pbk)
ISBN: 0-595-65525-4 (Cloth)

Printed in the United States of America

With gratitude,

I first dedicate this book to my three uncles,
who served in the U.S. Navy,

Charles Herbert McElroy,

The late Donald Henderson Johnson,

The late Cordon Merle Johnson

And to my sister, Rita Darlene Johnson Wartena,
who is a Naval Reservist and has been called to active duty twice in
her 20 year Naval Reserve career, the first time during Desert Storm
and the second time for security detail on the War on Terrorism

and to all veterans of the U.S. Naval services

past and present

for your undue loyalty and service in the protection of this great
country we call the

United States of America.

Contents

Introduction

This book was a dream that stayed with me for years. When I was given the inspiration to write another book, I then decided that this dream would have to become a reality, too.

During my 20 years in the Navy, I served on 5 different ships and was assigned to four different shore installations. I had seen all types of things that were humorous. I saw many things that could have turned out to be disastrous had it not been for the professionalism of those officers and sailors I served with. I saw things that were immoral and unethical with officers and/or enlisted involved.

I have heard Navy stories that go back as far as World War II. My idea 10 years ago was to write a book about my experiences and include stories from other sailors. I love sharing and telling stories and I know others love to listen to or read stories. So this book is for your enjoyment.

Some of the stories, especially in the chapters about "Great Navy Food" and "Drunken Sailors, Fighting Sailors", may not be to your liking but they may be for others. Just bypass those stories and read the others that are to your liking. In those chapters that I deem somewhat unfit for human consumption I have placed a warning at the beginning.

My stories will have some names; however, if I felt that the person would have been upset with me using his/her name, I used their rate or have changed the name to protect them. I have stayed away from naming people in the stories about Immoral and Unethical acts or situations. My intent is to let you know about some of those acts that do go on in the Navy, but not to harm the reputation of those individuals involved. I will however try to impugn the motives of those individuals without naming names. Impugn means to attack as false or questionable or to challenge in argument. This is my way of telling the Navy hierarchy that when allowed to rebut an adverse performance evaluation or fitrep that impugning the motives of those responsible should be allowed since that is what they did to you when they wrote the adverse performance evaluation or fitrep. Some of those people if they read this will know whom I am talking about and hopefully they will feel a bit of remorse or guilt about what happened.

Sit back, read, enjoy.

"Poor is the Nation that has no heroes. Shameful is the nation that having them, forgets." Author: Unknown

Prologue

I Am the American Sailor
By Anonymous
Contributed by Don Johnson

I Am the American Sailor—

Hear my voice, America! Though I speak through the mist of 200 years, my shout for freedom will echo through liberty's halls for many centuries to come.

Hear me speak, for my words are of truth and justice, and the rights of man. For those ideals, I have spilled my blood upon the world's troubled waters.

Listen well, for my time is eternal—yours is but a moment.

I am the spirit of heroes past and future. I am the American Sailor. I was born upon the icy shores at Plymouth, rocked upon the waves of the Atlantic, and nursed in the wilderness of Virginia.

I cut my teeth on New England codfish, and I was clothed in southern cotton.

I built muscle at the halyards of New Bedford whalers, and I gained my sea legs high atop the mizzen of Yankee clipper ships.

Yes, I am the American Sailor, one of the greatest seamen the world has ever known.

The sea is my home and my words are tempered by the sound of paddle wheels on the Mississippi, and the song of whales off Greenland's barren shore. My eyes have grown dim from the glare of sunshine on blue water, and my heart is full of star-strewn nights under the Southern Cross.

My hands are raw from winter storms while sailing-down around the Horn, and they are blistered from the heat of cannon broadsides while defending our nation.

I am the American Sailor, and I have seen the sunset of a thousand distant, lonely lands.

I am the American Sailor.

It was I who stood tall beside John Paul Jones as he shouted, "I have not yet begun to fight!"

I fought upon Lake Erie with Perry, and I rode with Stephen Decatur into Tripoli harbor to burn the Philadelphia.

I met Guerriere aboard Constitution, and I was lashed to the mast with Admiral Farragut at Mobile Bay.

I have heard the clang of Confederate shot against the sides of Monitor.

I have suffered the cold with Peary at the North Pole, and I responded when Dewey said, "You may fire when ready Gridley," at Manila Bay.

It was I who transported supplies through submarine infested waters when our soldier's were called "over there".

I was there as Admiral Byrd crossed the South Pole.

It was I who went-down with the Arizona at Pearl Harbor, who supported our troops at Inchon, and patrolled the dark deadly waters of the Mekong Delta.

I am the American Sailor, and I wear many faces. I am a pilot soaring across God's blue canopy, and I am a Seabee atop a dusty bulldozer in the South Pacific.

I am a corpsman nursing the wounded in the jungle, and I am a torpedoman in the Nautilus deep beneath the North Pole.

I am hard and I am strong.

But it was my eyes that filled with tears when my brother went-down with the Thresher, and it was my heart that rejoiced when Commander Shepherd rocketed into orbit above the earth.

It was I who languished in a Viet Cong prison camp, and it was I who walked upon the moon.

It was I who saved the Stark, and the Samuel B. Roberts in the mine infested waters of the Persian Gulf.

It was I who pulled my brothers from the smoke filled compartments of the Bonefish, and wept when my shipmates died on the Iowa, and White Plains.

When called again, I was there, on the tip of the spear for Operation Desert Shield, and Desert Storm.

I am the American Sailor.

I am woman, I am man, I am white and black, yellow, red and brown. I am Jew, Muslim, Christian, and Buddhist. I am Irish, Filipino, African, French, Chinese, and Indian.

And my standard is the outstretched hand of Liberty.

Today, I serve around the world; on land, in air, on and under the sea. I serve proudly, at peace once again, but with the fervent prayer that I need not be called again.

Tell your children of me.

Tell them of my sacrifice, and how my spirit soars above their country.

I have spread the mantle of my nation over the ocean, and I will guard her forever. I am her heritage, and yours.

I am the American Sailor.

I Am The American Sailor is believed to be a letter found on the steps leading to the Tomb of the Unknown Soldier.

The letter says it all about U.S. Navy sailors (officers and enlisted).

Chapter 1

Ships Passing in the Night (or Day)

An oiler refueling two ships at sea

The first chapter of this book has stories about two incidents that happened during my career and very much stayed with me for all of these years. Both incidents were very scary. The third story is about an incident witnessed by a fellow Radioman during and shortly after replenishment at sea off the coast of Vietnam. His story stayed with him until he sent it to me several months ago.

A Close Encounter in Vung Tau Harbor
By LT Don Johnson, USN (Ret), ex-RM1

My first time overseas in 1970 took me to places that only my uncles had talked about for many years. One place they never talked about was Vietnam.

The USS Guadalupe (AO-32), aka Greasy Guad, the second oldest ship in the Navy at the time, did its thing by traveling south to north and back again from the southern tip of South Vietnam around Anthoi Island to the Gulf of Tonkin. We would do ten days on the line refueling all types of ships, aircraft carriers, destroyers, cruisers, battleships, Coast Guard cutters, Australian destroyers and then dumping what we had left into a jumble oiler. After that it was back to Subic Bay for 3 days of fun and games.

One of the times that we were out on the line refueling ships, we made a brief stop in Vung Tau harbor at the mouth of the Mekong River.

Anytime that we pulled into port or anchored anywhere close to land in South Vietnam, we would have fifty calibers set up on the O-2 level (two levels above the main deck) just outside the radio shack and the Captain's Cabin. I prayed that we never got into a firefight where the enemy was firing back at us. Those thin bulkheads would not have stopped some of the bullets that the enemy was using.

This particular stop was a different one. The gunner's mates were told to be on the lookout for sampans trying to come close to the ship.

That kind of scared me.

When we pulled into the harbor that day, the Captain knew where he wanted to anchor and that was not in any of the specially designated anchor areas as noted on the charts that we had.

The radarmen (now Operations Specialists) and quartermasters told the Captain that this was not the place to anchor. The Captain said drop the anchor right here.

Everyone did as told.

USS Guadalupe (AO-32) at sea off the coast of Vietnam

We were anchored for a couple of hours. Then the XO began to get a little nervous about the sampans in the harbor. We tried our best to warn them to not come close. However, they were not the danger that day.

I was on watch in the radio shack and overheard the noise on one of the harbor circuits. The Operations Officer, I believe, was trying to talk to a freighter and trying to get it to shift course. This went on for quite some time maybe ten to fifteen minutes. That is a long time when you are trying to communicate with someone of a different nationality.

The next thing I heard was the sound of the general collision alarm. I ran outside the shack to see what was going on. What I saw was this huge freighter bearing down on us. They did not change course one bit. They kept coming and coming. They passed us by and I know that they missed our bow by just a few feet.

I also heard Radioman First Class Dan Daniels yelling at the freighter and shaking his fist. The freighter nearly messed up Dan's departure for home. He departed the ship during our next in port period to Subic.

The only thing I saw wrong with this picture was that the Captain had anchored in the middle of a sea-lane. The radarmen and quartermasters had tried to warn him.

If we had had a collision with that freighter, the Captain would have been responsible for the entire incident. By the grace of God that collision never happened.

Doesn't Anyone Listen to the Conning Officer?
By Don Johnson, LT, USN (Ret), ex-RM1

I was the conning officer on USS Belleau Wood (LHA-3) one night while out cruising east to west legs west of San Diego harbor. The Officer of the Deck (OOD) was the First Lieutenant, LCDR R.T. The commanding officer, Captain C.B. was also on the bridge.

Belleau Wood during flight operations

About 20 miles due west of the navigational sea buoy marked as 1SD is a rock that juts out from the bottom of the sea and is known as Bishop's Rock. It has a navigational light on it so you don't run into it.

Well, many a mariner have run into Bishop's Rock even USS Enterprise (CV-65). The Big E ran aground at Bishop's Rock not too long after it had gone aground in San Francisco Bay back in the 1980's.

Our CO had the Combat Information Center and the quartermasters (navigators) draw a five mile radius circle around Bishop's Rock so that we never came any closer than that.

On this particular night with me as conning officer on the 2000-2400 watch, we were doing east and west legs all night so that we would be close to port the next morning for some reason now that escapes me.

We were headed west on a 270 degree course. For all of you landlubbers, 000 degrees is due north, 090 degrees due east, 180 degrees due south, and 270 degrees due west. As I was watching the radar repeater I noticed a crossing situation behind us with a freighter heading into San Diego harbor and the USS Cape Cod coming out. The CO gave the order to reverse course and head back into San Diego.

I recommended to the OOD and the CO that we maintain our present course until the crossing situation was past and then reverse course.

The CO knew that staying on course would put us very close to the five mile radius of Bishop's Rock if we maintained our course. He said to reverse course. Being the obedient junior officer that I was, I gave the orders.

"Left standard rudder, come to course 090." The helmsman parroted my orders.

As we were coming around I noticed on the radar repeater that the Cape Cod had changed her course more to the south and increased her speed and crossed in front of the freighter which by nautical rules should have been a big no-no given the closeness of the crossing situation.

I told the OOD this and he looked at his radar repeater and told me that I was wrong.

I put my binoculars up to my eyes and looked and I saw the red running light of the Cape Cod and the green running light of the freighter, so I knew what I was looking at.

I told the OOD to look for himself. He did not.

I was doing my calculations on a mo-board and I saw what was going to happen if we did not come right to course 120 even if for just a short time. We were on a collision course with the Cape Cod.

I kept recommending to the OOD to come right to course 120 and I was not paying attention to what the helmsman was doing.

At one time during the course of this situation, I swear I heard the CO recommend to the OOD to come left to course 070; however, I never gave the orders to do so, because I knew I was right.

Within the next ten minutes while we were still coming around, I kept recommending that we change course to 120 because of the collision course we were on.

The Cape Cod kept coming and we kept going.

I kept watching the situation in my binoculars. Finally, I said out loud to the OOD so the CO could hear that we change course to 120.

I was not watching the gyro and we had already passed course 090 and was heading to course 070. I had forgotten to order the helmsman to steady up on course 090. So he did what he was supposed to do and that was to continue on. My original order was to come to course 090. I never told him to steady up on course 090. When you are reversing course, you normally do not tell the helmsman to steady up until you are within about twenty degrees of the course, or at least that is what I was taught by a couple of good OODs. I was so caught up in the crossing situation turned collision course situation that I forgot to tell him to steady on course 090. The helmsman should have been telling me every twenty degrees what was happening such as passing 250, passing 230, etc. That would have been a reminder to me. But that never happened.

The CO was looking through his binoculars by this time. When he finally realized what I was saying, he looked up and said, "Who in the hell gave the order to bring us to course 070?" I said, "You did, sir."

All of a sudden the OOD realized what was going on and turned and gave the following orders:

"This is Lieutenant Commander R.T. I am the Officer of the Deck and I have the conn. Hard right rudder. Belay all orders."

As we came back around to course 090 we continued on. We were still bearing down on the Cape Cod at ten knots who was bearing down on us at 15 knots. As we continued on around to course 120 the Cape Cod passed down our port side within 500 yards. We could see their bridge personnel standing on their port bridge wing.

After we passed the Cape Cod, the CO looked at the OOD and told him to get me off his bridge.

I had embarrassed him and almost caused a collision at sea between two large naval vessels. That would have been a career ending thing for him, the OOD and me.

I did find out later from the OOD that I was correct on all assumptions except the 070 order from the Captain. The quartermaster of the watch told me a few days later that the CO did recommend to the OOD that we come left to course 070, but the OOD recommended against it. I did not hear that and I guess I never gave the order to come to course 070.

That was when I sat back and wondered how we had come around to course 070 at the time the OOD took over the conn. My earlier details are what I remember happening.

Only the CO, the OOD, the bridge watch and I knew what happened that night. I continued on with my surface warfare officer training and completed 90% of it before I left Belleau Wood.

Replenishment off the Coast of Vietnam
By Bob Price

I first joined the Naval Reserves in Philadelphia in July of 1964. In February 1965, I joined the regular Navy and was sent to Bainbridge, MD for radioman "A" school. From there I was ordered to Yokosuka Japan for a two-year tour at the Naval Communication Station, arriving in early November 1965. As soon as I reported on board, I began volunteering for duty in Vietnam. I tried to get into ACB-1, Beach Masters, SEALS, UDT or anything I could to get "In-Country". I have always been a history nut and grew up with the stories of WWII from my father and others in the neighborhood. In any event, I finally was selected for duty in Can Tho and, after training in the Philippines I arrived in early February 1966. We were officially attached to Headquarters, Support Activity, Saigon, but while in Can Tho, we were paid by the Army and attached to Advisory Team 96. We set up communication vans at the Can Tho airfield next to a Special Forces command. We also began to construct docks at a South Vietnamese Naval facility near the mouth of the Bassac River for Operation Game Warden. The first Mark 1 PBR's (Patrol Boat, River) arrived in early May 1966 and river operations began almost immediately. I left Vietnam in June 1966 and returned to Yokosuka to complete my tour.

In November 1967, I received orders for the USS Annapolis (AGMR-1) for a one-year tour of duty operating mostly in the Gulf of Tonkin. There were two communication and command ships (AGMRs) at the time; The Annapolis and the Arlington and they operated on a "blue & gold" schedule. One communication ship had to be on Yankee Station at all times. In early 1968, we had just been relieved by the Arlington and were on our way to Australia when the North Koreans captured the USS Pueblo and we immediately returned to the line as the Arlington was ordered to accompany the USS Enterprise and her task force to Korean waters. We spent a total of 70 days at sea on that occasion.

USS Annapolis (AGMR-1) at sea somewhere in the Western Pacific

The short story I mentioned occurred during an "un-rep" with one of the hospital ships (either the USS Repose or the USS Sanctuary). We had all the lines, hoses, and bosun chairs in place and were standing on the antenna deck staring almost in disbelief at actual American Nurses; a very rare site anywhere in the Far East but to see so many in the middle of the ocean, was unbelievable. (As you probably know, any American women were known affectionately as "round-eyes".) Anyway, we were all jammed on the starboard side of the ship trying to converse with the nurses as they were connected to each other, a distance of no more than 30 feet if that, when suddenly a bunch of dust-off choppers came in low and fast. There wasn't time to consider disconnecting the lines and hoses as the helicopters were circling all around both ships. None of us on the Annapolis understood what was happening but each chopper was loaded with severely wounded Marines. We could hear the screaming and, my first impression was they must have been doused with oil or something like that because their fatigues appeared black! All of a sudden, all of the nurses white uniforms began to turn red and we realized that the fatigues were soaked with blood. As the wounded Marines were all off one chopper, the gunner tossed off body parts just before taking off so another one could land. This continued until all of the helicopters were unloaded. There must have been over 30 Marines or perhaps an entire platoon and all were extreme cases. I am assuming they were Marines as we were not too far off the coast and it was in a Marine area of operations (I Corps).

What I remember the most was watching the nurses uniforms turn to bright red before my eyes. I also seem to remember the corpsmen and/or Doctors tossing the body parts over the side but I was over 30 feet away and could not swear to that. At the time, I believed that the arms and legs were too badly mangled to be re-attached. This was a long time ago, but sometimes it seems like yesterday.

Chapter 2

The Perfect Storm

The movie, "The Perfect Storm", may have been the perfect storm for that small fishing boat, but many Navy ships have been through similar storms and to the sailors who rode out those storms probably felt that had just experienced "The Perfect Storm". Every ship that I had been stationed on for more than 60 days had been through "The Perfect Storm" and I have lived through each one of them to tell about them.

Stormy seas

Sit back, read and ride out the storms with me.

Super Typhoon Pamela—1976
By Don Johnson, LT, USN (Ret), ex-RM1

I had just reported to the USS Peoria in April 1976. I had re-enlisted after having been out for 2 1/2 years going to college, working odd jobs and trying to raise a family. I did not want to go back out to sea and be away from my family, but this was the Navy way. Go to sea to get that needed promotion.

I re-enlisted on March 31, 1976 and the Peoria set sail for a Western Pacific deployment on April 9, 1976. I did not have time to get my family settled as my pregnant wife and oldest daughter were living with her parents until I could muster enough money to send her for an apartment.

On our way over we stopped in Hawaii to pick up a company of Marines and their AAVs (amphibious tanks) and then headed to Guam our next port of call. We knew there was a storm brewing east-southeast of Guam because of the weather reports coming in via the Navy communications systems broadcast. Our ship's navigator began tracking the storm. The storm went from a tropical depression to a tropical storm to a full fledged typhoon in four days. As the storm tracked to the west-northwest, it appeared that it was going to track south of Guam and miss it.

We pulled into Guam towards the beginning of May. I dropped off half of my teletypes to the ship repair facility for maintenance since we did not have a full time teletype repairman. RMC (Chief Radioman) was the Chief Master at Arms and spent most of his time doing those duties. He would spend some time working on the teletypes when he had the time. We were now partying down at the Enlisted club the first night and got into a confrontation with some Marines on the bus taking us back to the ship. You can hear about that one in a later story.

The next morning or the second day in, we were told by port authorities that we may have to lift anchor and leave the next day because the storm had changed its track and was headed straight towards Guam. I began tracking the storm myself as I pulled the weather messages off the broadcast skeds. I delivered the messages to the Command Duty Officer. By that second evening in port we knew that we were going to have to depart the next morning in order to ride the storm out.

As we were preparing to leave the next morning, I had radiomen begin to tie things down so that they did come loose and hurt someone. I also had a rack of test equipment that we used to test and synchronize the receive signals of the Navy's radio teletype broadcast. In this rack was a signal generator, a huge 24"X24"X24" oscilloscope, and a few other smaller pieces of test equipment. I began using the equipment on the way over from San Diego because we had some of the worst kept receivers and multiplexers in the Navy. I had to learn to use the equipment so that we did not miss too many Navy messages.

We got underway in the early afternoon with only half of my teletypes. My Chief assured me that we would be back to pick them up.

To tell you a little more about the Peoria, it was a Newport-class LST with a flat-bottom and a bow horn that supported the bow ramp that stuck out like a rhino's horn. Before we left San Diego we embarked an amphibious Seabee unit that brought with them four 10' x 75' causeways or floating pontoon bridges that would be hooked together to make one fairly long bridge from our bow ramp to the beach.

As we headed to the southwest of Guam the waters began to get somewhat choppy. Into the second and third days it was really rough. I went up to the signal bridge where I hung out with a couple of signalmen. I can't recall their names. I stood up front on the signal bridge and watched the waters. We were taking waves that had to be at least 20 foot coming over the bow of the ship.

By this time many of the Marines and a majority of the crew were seasick. I was close to being seasick, but I just kept eating crackers and drinking 7Up. I tried to sleep that night, but the waves were lifting up the causeways and then they would crash back against the side of the ship. I couldn't sleep. I decided to go back up to the radio shack since I had the mid-watch.

I had a seasick sailor in secure teletype trying to keep the broadcast going. He was so sick that he was unable to find the best frequency for the broadcast which we were picking up from Guam. I began searching for a frequency and could not find a decent one, so I decided to check on frequencies out of Hawaii. I found a couple and began copying that broadcast and sent out a message via ship to shore radio that I was shifting my communications guard to Hawaii since I was unable to communicate with Guam. After the broadcast stabilized, I decided to sit down in the supervisor's chair and relax a while. The ship was taking rolls at about 30-40 degrees, so I was sitting there letting the rolls shift me back and forth in the chair. Sometimes the rolls would lift the front chair legs off the floor and I would roll back a little more. This kept up for about an hour or so, then the ship took a 40 plus degree roll to starboard and as it did my chair came back and I did not catch it in time and I landed flat on my back under the test equipment rack. Just as I pulled myself up, we took another 40 plus degree roll to port and at that time the fifty pound 24" cube oscilloscope broke its mountings and came crashing down to the floor in the exact same place my head had been just seconds before. It was broken, and now I would not have the piece of test equipment to tweak my frequencies. I did not think about it until the next day when it hit me that if I had stayed on the floor any longer than I did that I may not have made it back to Guam. That test equipment probably would have killed me.

Once my watch relief came in the morning, I went down for a little breakfast of toast and coffee. Since I could not sleep, I went back up to the signal bridge for a while and had a hard time making it to the signal bridge house. We were taking waves over the top of the bow horn which was about forty feet above the water line. By afternoon we had taken some waves up over the signal bridge which is about 60 feet above the water line.

I still could not sleep so I went down to the radio shack to help out with communications and keeping my guys going. At this time we were about three days out of Guam; and we noticed that Typhoon Pamela had become a level 5 typhoon and was renamed Super Typhoon Pamela. She was charting a course that would take her right over the top of Guam with 200mph winds.

As the next day or so went on the waves began to die down. Our communications with Hawaii were there, but not as well as we wanted them. We knew that we were not going to be talking with Guam until we pulled back into port.

We heard that after Super Typhoon Pamela had passed, that they had lost all communications with the outside world except for one trans-Pacific cable with Hawaii and that it was not in very good condition. All of their transmitting and receiving antennas were either damaged beyond use or gone. Their satellite terminals were all but gone, the same ones that I had worked with when I was stationed their three years before.

Nearly 80% of all housing was either destroyed or damaged. As we pulled back into port, we noticed that all trees were blown over or if they had not blown over were bare of leaves. It looked as though an atomic bomb had leveled the island. You could not believe the damage unless you saw it.

We ended up staying there for the next six weeks and provided power and water to the Naval Station. We also provided communications support to the Naval Station through Hawaii.

Did I learn something? You bet I did. I learned that life is very precious and that sometimes Mother Nature will take life away.

I also learned that you should brag a little more about what you do and then maybe you will get recognized. It was my idea to shift our communications guard to Hawaii and maintain a ship to shore radio termination for a few weeks. I never got credit for that. My Chief received a Navy Achievement Medal for my idea. All I got was a Meritorious Unit Commendation along with all the other sailors who were a part of the island cleanup. Am I still mad? Not anymore. My Navy career turned out to be very rewarding with many lessons learned.

A Challenge to Change Home Ports
By Don Johnson, LT, USN (Ret), ex-RM1

USS Belleau Wood (LHA-3) was tired and ready for an overhaul. Her overhaul was going to be done at the Puget Sound Naval Shipyard in Bremerton, Washington.

Our transit to Bremerton from San Diego was uneventful. However, the next ten months would be very eventful.

Everyone was moved off the ship into barracks ashore or in my case I bought a house and moved the family up from San Diego.

We had a berthing barge moved to the other side of the pier from us so that the watch section could reside there on duty days.

During the first week in drydock, I had the 2000-2400 watch on the quarterdeck which was set up on the hangar deck back near the port elevator.

Around 2100, I smelled what appeared to be diesel fuel. All of a sudden one of the shipyard workers came running over to the quarterdeck yelling that we were pumping fuel into the drydock.

I ran over to the starboard side where we had a brow set up to let ship-yard workers onboard. The worker who warned us pointed down to bottom of the drydock and sure enough we were pumping DFM over the side into the drydock.

I immediately ran back over to the quarterdeck and took the 1MC into my hands and passed the word to stop all pumping. I had my messenger of the watch go over to the starboard brow and watch and to let me know when pumping had ceased. I tried calling the duty engineer of the watch to determine what was going on. I got a hold of him and I told him that they were pumping fuel over the side and he said that he was not. I told him that they were and to stop all pumping.

I also called away the in port fire party just in case that fuel sparked a fire since it was being pumped and landing near live electrical outlets. I wanted to be prepared.

Our CO had returned from some social function only 30 minutes before and called down to find out what was going on.

When I told him, he wanted the duty engineer of the watch in his inport cabin as soon as the pumping ceased.

It was not a pretty sight the next morning. KING-TV had a helicopter flying near the base showing the 5,000 gallon oil slick that was coming from our drydock.

Not a good way to start an overhaul.

The overhaul did not start out too good for me either, but it did allow me to re-group so I could begin to prepare for the next year's selection board.

One of our brand new ensigns went away to Surface Warfare Officer School. He went home to get married and then lost his new wife in a boating accident on Lake Shasta.

It was not a very good year all the way around for us.

Captain was determined to get us out of the yards on time. Most big ships that go into overhaul end up getting extended for some reason or another. Our CO was not going to allow that to happen. He kept us all focused on our goal of coming out of the overhaul on time. Guess what? We did.

As we prepared to leave Bremerton, we took as many of the ship's crew's vehicles on board and as many families as we could to save the Navy bundles of money in moving expenses. I elected to leave my family in Bremerton because I felt that I could somehow talk my way into a duty station up there. As it turned out later it did not happen.

We left Bremerton the morning of January 28th. Everyone on board who had families in San Diego or who had families on board for the transit south where rejoicing in the fact that we were leaving Bremerton.

But as we transited the Straits of San Juan de Fuca, we had the Challenger shuttle launch on CCTV. Many of us watched as the space shuttle blew up. That set the tone for the rest of the trip south.

Space Shuttle Challenger before explosion

I had not paid any attention to the weather reports. The closer we got to California the worst the weather was getting.

When I finally started paying attention to the weather reports, I noticed that they were saying this storm was not a hurricane or a tropical storm.

It had a very wide swath. It had a low pressure center that looked like the eye of a hurricane and it had winds packing at 70 miles per hour. Now doesn't that sound like a hurricane or a tropical storm to you?

We continued south and as we did I would go up to the signal bridge to see what was going on.

The weather was just plain nasty and they were passing the word to stay off all weather decks.

My 35 foot whip antennas along the forward port and starboard flight deck were beginning to feel the brunt of those 70 mph winds. A couple of them began to work themselves loose. I noticed one on the starboard side that appeared to be ready to fall off and fall over the side. I called down to radio and told them to get someone out to tie that antenna down so we did not lose it.

We had 70 mph winds coming across the flight deck. Waves were white-caps and they were huge. Every now and then we would hit a trough and a wave would come crashing over the top of the bow which sits about 65 feet above the water line.

Finally a couple of my radiomen and one of my chiefs got out on the catwalk where that antenna was located. They determined what they needed to tie it down. They also had on safety harnesses and would attach themselves to a stanchion or a lifeline so that if one of those waves hit them they would not be washed overboard. Trying to rescue someone in those kinds of conditions would have been almost next to impossible.

The chief and radiomen finally had all the tools they needed to secure the antenna and did so. We also found out that the antennas would probably survive better if we raised them to the vertical position instead of the horizontal as they were. The waves that were coming up over the bow were playing havoc with the horizontal antennas. The vertical position put them in a better position away from the waves, but then the winds pushed their limits.

We left them in the vertical position until we got through the storm.

I do not remember who the two radiomen and the chief were that went out there to secure the antennas, but they were brave in my eyes. All it would have taken was one incorrect move and I could have lost three of my men.

Someday I may remember who they were. I can see their faces, but I cannot remember their names.

<u>Making Love to a Chair</u>
By Don Johnson, LT, USN (Ret)

I had reported on board USS Belleau Wood (LHA 3) at sea three days out of Hong Kong after spending three weeks in Subic Bay waiting for the ship to pull in port. I could not get any information from base operations on her whereabouts or when she was going to pull in port.

I finally made it to the Naval Communications Station at San Miguel and met up with an old friend who got me the information I needed. As soon as I got the information, we sent a Naval message to the ship requesting transportation for me to meet the ship in Okinawa. I was bored and wanted to get to the ship to begin my new job.

Air transportation was provided to Okinawa and then I caught USS Dubuque who was going to meet up with Belleau Wood before Hong Kong. When Dubuque met up with the B-Wood, a helo was sent over to pick up passengers. I had spent three boring days on Dubuque.

When I got on board, I met up with the LT that I was relieving and the RMCS who I had been stationed with for 9 of my 34 months in Hawaii. RMCS and I did not get along too well in Hawaii. We were both RM1s together and had our own ideas how to run the Fleet Telecommunications Operations Center. He managed a particular part of the center and was also the leading petty officer. When he left, I took his job for the remainder of the time I was there.

He went to the B-Wood and made Chief and Senior Chief. I was selected for the limited duty officer program. Now I was an officer and he a Senior Chief.

I got settled in over the next few days. I was assigned a stateroom with the intelligence officer (cryptology).

While in port Hong Kong I went over and bought a few items to send home to Barbara.

When we left Hong Kong it was back to Subic Bay for a few days before heading off to Singapore where I played golf with one of the RM1s and was offered a marijuana joint by my caddy. I quickly turned him down and told him that I did not smoke that stuff.

Later that night the RM1 and I met up with several Radiomen from the ship and sat around on Boogie Street drinking beer and yelling obscenities to the transvestites who hung around to see if they could lure some young sailor into their clutches for the rest of the evening.

After Singapore it was off to Phuket Island, Thailand. I had been to Pattaya Beach on the opposite coast several years before and loved it. I had purchased my wife a blue star sapphire ring.

Phuket was different. It was a resort island where many Europeans came to vacation. Patong Beach had several nude beaches that the Europeans visited.

We anchored off Patong Beach the first day. We had a real problem with the weather and the waves, so the next morning the ship lifted anchor and moved to the opposite side of the island off Phuket (the city) itself. I had duty that first day so I was involved with the moving of the ship. I had the next three days off.

During those three days I partied with Andy, my CMS Custodian. We got us a bungalow and drank and walked the streets of Patong Beach and drank and walked and drank and ate lots of seafood pizza one of the delicacies of Patong Beach.

The morning we pulled out to head to Australia I came down with some type of stomach ailment probably from the raw seafood on the pizza.

During the trip south to Australia I practically lived in the head. I had my favorite commode. I also hoarded rolls of toilet paper so if we ran short at least I would have my stash.

The trip south to Fremantle, Australia took seven days. We pulled into port to pick up some Australian Navy and Marines to participate in an exercise with us. We were there for less than two days. After the completion of the exercise we would be pulling back into Fremantle for seven days.

The day we pulled out of port the weather was getting a little rough. We were doing east and west legs. The seas were getting pretty high during the second day out with the waves topping out at 25'.

We were taking 15-20 degree rolls with some of them hitting about 30. I stayed up until about 2300 the second night out. My roommate, the Intel officer, was already in his top rack fast asleep.

I got into my bottom rack and laid there for about half an hour before I fell asleep. At about 0100 we took a tremendous roll and I heard something sliding across our room. My desk chair that had not been tied down came sliding across the room and landed in the rack with me. I was somewhat taken aback. I am fighting the chair and trying to get it out of the rack when my roommate woke up, turned his bunk light on and asked what I was doing. I said, "What does it look like? I am making love to my chair. This chair would not take 'no' for an answer."

I finally was able to push the chair back out of the bunk. I got up and called up to Radio to find out if someone knew how big a roll we took. The radio supervisor did not know, so he called the Signal Shack who told him that we had just taken a 37 degree roll. Now that is a roll for a big ship! Rumor had it that the superstructure was built to withstand a 45 degree roll before it broke off and fell into the sea. That is coming pretty close.

I guess what really happened was that we were in heavy seas and when we turned 180 degrees to head back into land one of the waves caught us just as we were parallel with it forcing us into that 37 degree roll.

There were many things that had broken loose from their tie downs especially Marine equipment in the well deck and in the hangar deck.

The next day the weather began to taper off and we were able to continue on with the exercise and eventually pulled back into port where we spent seven wonderful days.

Don't Mess with the Indy, Saddam
By Don Johnson, LT, USN (ret)

The day was August 2. The USS Independence (CV-62) had just transited the Malacca Straits a few days before and was a week out of Diego Garcia for an operational exercise. I was the Assistant Communications Officer/Radio Officer onboard.

On that morning, Rear Admiral Unruh received a secure conference call from Commander in Chief Pacific Fleet and Central Command in MacDill.

Iraq had just invaded Kuwait. Intelligence sources were showing that Iraq had intended to invade the oil fields of Northern Saudi Arabia once they had secured Kuwait.

Our orders were to head north to the Gulf of Oman and to be on station within 48 hours to launch combat air patrols to protect Saudi Arabia. We were 1500 miles away. That meant that we had to do 30 plus knots to be on station to launch aircraft.

We headed north and in our way was a strong Indian Ocean storm. We had to go right through the middle of it. This storm had 30-40 foot seas.

As we headed north at 33 knots we could see the seas becoming very choppy. About 6-8 hours into the transit the waves became white capped. I don't remember how high the waves were, but I know they were high enough to reach the old gun sponsons (former anti-aircraft gun emplacements) on the port and starboard sides of the carrier. They were about 40 feet above sea level. These gun sponsons were being pummeled by the waves.

The signal bridge was also one of my responsibilities. I would go up and sit and talk to the SM1 (I think his first name was Cliff) and SMCM (SW) Jim Comstock. I noticed the smaller ships were having real problems with the weather. The waves were continuously traveling over the bow of the ships as we headed north at a high rate of speed.

We entered the storm at about six hours into the transit and exited it about 18 hours later.

We arrived on station on time and launched a combat air patrol (CAP) over Northern Saudi Arabia to deter the Iraqi military from coming across the border from Kuwait.

Inspection of the ship showed the forward gun sponsons were heavily damaged from the heavy seas that we taken on. These sponsons originally were concaved outward and made of ¾" thick aluminum. The concave shape of the forward gun sponsons were smashed inward.

If water can travel that high and damage that thickness of aluminum, you know we were in one heck of a storm.

And once again, Saddam, we, the crew of the Indy and its fire power, kept our date and kept you from terrorizing another nation.

That Antenna Can Wait
By Don Johnson, LT, USN (Ret), ex-RM1

When you are a young 18 year old, you sometimes do not fear anything.

USS Guadalupe (AO-32) was off the coast of Southern California doing work ups prior to leaving on a deployment to Vietnam.

This could have been during refresher training or it could have been during one of our other training evolutions. The type of evolution is vague in my mind but the incident that I am about to tell you about is as fresh in my mind as if it happened yesterday.

During this at sea period the seas became somewhat rough. Being a deep draft ship you did not feel as much of the rock and roll as maybe a destroyer or cruiser.

The winds picked up and before too long we had gale force winds of 40 knots coming across the bow of the ship.

Someone came into the radio shack and said that the starboard section glass insulator of the long-wire receive antenna had come loose from one of its couplings. This antenna was made up of one long copper wire which was fed back and forth through glass insulators with each insulator attached to a coupling device to keep it secure. Four of the glass insulators were secured to coupling devices 12" apart on the electronics repair shack and then routed into our radio shack and into a radio frequency (RF) receiving coupler. The other ends of the antenna array were stretched aft to the amidships mast starting at the center of the mast and the starboard side yardarm, attached to a glass insulator that was attached to a coupling device about three feet away and then fed over to another glass insulator, secured and then fed down to the electronic repair shack and back up to the mast. This was done four times placing the starboard section at the far starboard side of the mast.

Someone was going to have to go up the amidships mast and try to secure it to the yardarm.

All of us radiomen went out to look at the flailing antenna segment. At the time I was the youngest of the radiomen being only 18 years old. Most of the other guys had either been in the Navy for quite some time or were quite a bit older than me when they joined the Navy. And what I mean by a quite a bit older than me I mean 3-5 years older.

The Chief wanted someone to go up and try to grab it and secure it to the yardarm. All of them looked at me. I told them that I wasn't going up there by myself.

Well, an RM1 to be left nameless spoke up and said that if I went up there with him and held a safety line, that he would go out on the yardarm, try to grab it and then secure it.

This RM1 was the residence drunk while inport. He went to the club, got drunk and came back to sleep off the drunkenness in the PO1 lounge.

Everyone looked at him like he was crazy. I thought he was too, but at least he was willing to try. Something had to happen before the antenna was damaged more and before someone was hurt by the swaying glass insulator.

RM1 put on a safety belt (we did not have safety harnesses back then). All we had for a safety line was some heavy duty twine.

We went outside and the wind was blowing very strong across the bow. The quartermasters said the wind indicators showed 42 knots. The sea was washing up into the tank deck which was just below the main deck.

We took the catwalk back from the forward superstructure to amidships and went a few more steps to the port side where the amidships mast was located.

RM1 began his climb up the 40' mast with me right behind him. If he had fallen, he would have knocked me off the mast and both of us would have been seriously injured.

Once at the top, RM1 saw that the port section and mid section of the antenna array were still securely tightened to their couplings so he took a chance and tightrope walked out onto the first section of the antenna array while holding onto handles that were positioned about every 18" along the top of the yardarm. He then slid his right leg up onto the yardarm and pulled himself around so he was sitting on the yardarm. I had somewhat secured the twine to a cleat that was welded to the side of the mast and as he walked out I was letting it follow him and keeping it taut at the same time.

The wind was blowing worse at the top of the mast than it was down below, because the ship's superstructure had been blocking some of the wind.

The wind was his biggest enemy as he was slowing inching his way out to the end of the yardarm, he almost slipped and fell. He had begun to slide around to the underside of the yardarm. He was able to grab one of the handles on the yardarm and pulled himself back onto the top of the yardarm. If he had fallen, I know I could have not held the 200 pound man and even if I could the wind was his biggest enemy. He would have been seriously injured if not killed.

RM1 finally had edged out to the end of the yardarm. The wind was blowing the starboard array all over the place. The glass insulator was violently flailing around from the 40 knot winds. If the glass insulator on the end of that array had hit him in the head, he would have fallen for sure.

Somehow (and today I would have to say that God helped us) he grabbed the glass insulator. He pulled some twine through the coupling at the end of the insulator and then tied it securely to the yardarm.

He then inched his way back and then stepped onto the port section of the antenna array. Once he got back to my position on the small platform at the middle of the yardarm, we both climbed down.

We both were cold, wet and tired from the ordeal. RM1 went down to his rack and I went into the radio shack. The Chief told me that neither of us really had to go up there since it was a dangerous evolution. I was mad at him. The other guys just kind of smirked at me knowing I was still a naïve young sailor. One day I would show them.

You want to talk about a storm. Try doing what we did in 40 knot winds 40 feet above a steel deck.

Chapter 3

Practical Jokes

Sailors are known for playing practical jokes on each other.

I was a gullible young sailor when I first went in the Navy and it stayed with me until the Guadalupe.

I have a few stories about practical jokes. Read and laugh. Some of the jokes may have been played on you.

Fallopian Tubes Onboard the Guad
By Don Johnson, LT, USN (Ret)-ex-RM1

When you first report to a ship right out of boot camp or Class "A" school, you are probably on of the most naïve and gullible sailors around. Your more experienced shipmates will try to find out how far you will go with practical joking.

I reported to the Guadalupe (AO-32) out of Radioman "A" school. The ship was in Bethlehem Steel shipyard undergoing an overhaul that would take her another five years down the road. She was already 31 years old, the second oldest ship in the Navy behind the Dixie.

I knew very little about most of the antiquated equipment since I had trained on the newer stuff in "A" school. One of the transmitters was as big as a small walk-in closet while another one was the oldest trans-ceiver that the Navy had in operation. They did get in the newest of transmitters and transceivers while in the yards which made things a lit-tle easier later on.

One of the pieces of equipment that I had never seen before was a tele-type signal converter call an AN/SGC-1A. I was given the responsibility of doing preventive maintenance (PMS) on this wicked piece of equip-ment. It gave me one of the good shocks of my life as you will read in the chapter on Shocking Stories.

After I received that shock, I told one of the three RM1s about it shock-ing me. I believe it was Dan Daniels. He did not say anything other than be careful and read the maintenance instructions really close the next time.

A day or two later, Dan came up to me and told me to take a supply requisition (Form 1250) down to GSK or general storekeeping to pick up a fallopian tube for the AN/SGC-1A because he thought that was the reason why I received that shock. Being the naïve seaman that I was, I took the 1250 down to GSK and handed it to SK2 Jones. I don't remember Jones' first name, but I do remember his last.

Jones actually took the 1250 from me and went to look to see if we had one in stock. He came back and told me that he did not think we carried such an item, but he would continue to look. I told him that RM1 Daniels told me that we carried those on board. I finally was tired of waiting so I told Jones that I would be back in a couple of hours to pick it up.

On my way back to Radio, I had a hunch that maybe Dan was playing games with me. I went down to the Ship's Office and asked to borrow a dictionary. When I found fallopian in there, I became angry, but then thought, let's continue to play the game.

When I got up to Radio, Dan asked me if GSK was able to locate that fallopian tube for the AN/SGC-1A. I told him that Jones was still searching. I told Dan that Jones had a lot of respect for him and his knowledge of what we were supposed to have carried on board. Dan thought I was joking and called GSK on one of the sound powered phone systems to find out if Jones was in fact still searching. When he found that Jones was still searching, he told him that he forgot that he used the last one a while back and forgot to reorder it. That resulted in no embarrassment on Jones' part.

Dan looked at me and asked me if I knew what it was and I told him that I knew all along what it was. I lied to him, but he had sent me on a wild goose chase, too. That was the last time anyone onboard the Guad sent me after a phony part.

I was still kind of the laughing stock of the radio shack. They all considered me a naïve young sailor and they thought I was a cry baby when I did not get my way. I probably was at that time. I was a very immature young man. I was learning quickly, though.

RM1 Robert "Vic" Ficarra became my mentor and the person I could go talk to when I had a problem with the guys.

Joking Sailors
By Don Johnson, LT, USN (Ret), ex-RM1

There were so many practical jokes that we pulled on other sailors over the years.

There were times that we would take a boot sailor and have him go down to general storekeeping (GSK) to get a gallon of bulkhead remover. Now how are you going to remove a steel bulkhead?

How about having them pick up a quart of stanchion grease? What stanchion are you going to grease up? Let's keep your minds out of the gutter.

A common one would be to send a brand new deck seaman to GSK to pick up 100 feet of chow line.

Radiomen had their own practical jokes. I was a teletype repairman during my second enlistment.

As we typed up naval messages, we had to type two carriage returns and one line feed at the end of each line.

After receiving some new radiomen onboard, I would come in to the secure teletype room and watch the Navy broadcast and when it hit reruns, I would release the teletype paper roller mechanism and then it would type over and over on the same line.

I would come back in and look at the broadcast and point it out to the new radioman and then immediately send him to GSK to get me some carriage returns and a line feed. They would look at me puzzled and I would tell them that I don't keep spares in my parts bin and that they had to go to GSK to get them. They would go and then come back up red faced and begin to call me some very common four letter words. I would just smile and leave after I had put the teletype back into normal operation.

Another thing I would do is to take two ply teletype paper and roll back the top layer of paper and tear if off so that the carbon paper would be showing.

I would then go to a new radioman and show him the roll of teletype paper and tell him that we were down to the last roll of two ply teletype paper and that we had no more on board. I would tell them that this roll was evidently put together wrong because the carbon paper was on top and the bottom two layers were standard teletype paper. I would ask them to find a way to get the carbon paper back between the bottom two layers.

Every time I did this, I watched them as they rolled the paper out in the passageways and then at the end of the roll, tear them off and then they would place the bottom layer of the roll on top of the carbon paper and then begin to roll it back up. It never dawned on them to just unroll the roll just enough, pull the bottom layer back around to the top and rip off the top 18-24" of the roll. I just thought it was comical and once they were done rolling it back up, I grabbed another two ply roll and showed them what I had done. Again four letter names graced the passageways of the ship.

Another old practical joke that goes way back is the sea bat.

This is always done at night. Everybody knows that sea bats don't come out during the daytime!

The Sea Bat is an ancient tradition. The perpetrators gather around a closed cardboard box and look hard at it. Many of them are leaning on brooms or swabs (mops to you landlubbers). There is often a piece of invisible fishing line running into the box tied to a bolt or something. One of the perpetrators is wiggling the line to make the bolt in the box make a little noise. Along comes the victim. Curiosity will make the person wonder what is in the box. "A Sea Bat" is the answer. Very rare creature. Mean sucker, too! No, you don't want to see it! I told you they're really mean. No, really, you DON'T want to open that box. Trust me! Oh, man! You're braver than I am! You get the idea. They'll say anything to keep the poor guy interested!

By this time, the victim has just GOTTA see this Sea Bat! When he bends over to open the box, all those brooms and swabs come up (just in case that thing gets loose, of course). When the box is opened, it's time to·strike! WHACK-O! All those brooms and swabs right on the victim's butt—he's just been bitten by a Sea Bat!

How about putting someone on a mail buoy watch? When you pull into Hong Kong and moor, you let the young sailors know that the mail is delivered to a buoy that we are moored to by a mail taxi and then we have to go pick it up. So you set up a watch schedule and have them standing on the bow of the ship watching the mooring buoy for mail. After they hear mail call, they know they have been had and once again curse words flow from their mouths.

If you don't have a good sense of humor, you will not have a good time at sea.

Marines at Sea
By Don Johnson, LT, USN (Ret), ex-RM1

The Peoria was my favorite duty station ever and that is probably because I was well known and got along with "just" about everyone.

I used to like to have fun with the Marines when they embarked.

Sailors very seldom get seasick because they get used to it after the first couple of times out to sea. I did have a young lad that got sick every time we pulled out to sea. It seemed that each time we unmoored from the pier he was sick. Almost every time for the first six months I would let him go down to see Doc and then hit his rack. It got to be a real nuisance after a while.

One time when we were pulling out, he wanted to go down to see Doc and then go hit his rack. We were short handed this time, so I told him NO! I gave him a clear plastic bag and told him to sit there and check the fleet broadcast and when he had to puke, to puke in the bag and when he got off watch, go outside, throw the bag over the side and then go down to hit his rack.

That seemed to do the trick. He very seldom got seasick after that, because he knew I would not let him leave.

When Marines embarked, there would be a number of them getting seasick and puking on our freshly cleaned decks.

Being the likeable guy that I was, when I caught Marines puking on my decks, I would tell them they had to clean up their own mess. They would plead to me to let them go to their berthing compartment. I threatened them with a report chit and Office Hours (Marine Captain's

Mast or non-judicial punishment). They always cleaned up their messes.

When it came time for meals, watch reliefs got priority in line. That included Marines. After all the watch reliefs got through the line, then it was a sailor and a marine alternately allowed into the chow line.

Once I was sitting and eating my chow and a couple of Marines came in and sat down. We were taking some good rolls. These two Marines got up to go get some bug juice or milk or something. When they got up they asked me to watch their trays.

I did watch their trays. As we took a good size roll to the starboard, their trays slid off the table and crashed onto the floor. They came back over and yelled at me for not watching their trays. I told them that I had watched their trays. I watched them slide off the table. I almost had to get up and defend my integrity until one of the sergeants came over to stop them from jumping on me.

Another thing I would do would be stand in line with my friends and we would all want to sit together at the same table. Many times we would not be able to because the Marines had taken up many of the seats.

One time we went into the dining facility and there were hardly any seats. The Marines had most of them and they were just sitting around chewing the fat. One of my buddies had mentioned loudly that some of them should get up and let us sit down. When they didn't, I said, "Watch this."

I sat down at a table that had one seat left. All the Marines were through, but were just sitting there talking.

I began to eat my spaghetti. When I had a mouthful, I feigned a stomach ache and said out loud that I was going to puke. I spit the spaghetti out, took my fork, played with it and then just prior to picking the spaghetti back up with my fork said, "Tastes better second time around." I began to eat the spaghetti that I had just spit out and you talk about Marines leaving in a hurry. I know they went to get rid of their lunch.

When they were all gone, I said, "Hey guys, plenty of seating here."

My buddies and I had a marvelous time eating and talking about the not so macho Marines.

Chapter 4

Shocking Tales

Sailors especially those in the more technical ratings such as Radioman, Electronics Technician and Electricians Mate work with a lot of high-powered electrical devices and sometimes during the course of doing preventive maintenance there is a high risk of electrical shock.

Personally I had three good shocks in twenty years of service. Sit back and read the shocking tales of sailors doing preventive maintenance on electrical/electronic equipment.

My Brush with Death from a Gibson Girl
By Steven Hawkins, ex-RM2 (SS)

Gibson Girl—NOUN: The American young woman of the 1890s as idealized in sketches by the American illustrator Charles Dana Gibson (1867–1944).

We had a girl on board my submarine when I was in the Navy. In fact we had two of them. They were Gibson Girls. They were not what you think. They were emergency lifeboat transmitters so named because of their hourglass shape. They were a bright yellow metal box with an hourglass shape so that they could be held tightly between your legs when in use. Inside was a radio transmitter powered by a generator that was powered by you, cranking on a hand crank that stuck out of the top. They came in a compact little kit, complete with an antenna and a kite to carry it up. There were also two balloons and the means to inflate them with hydrogen should there be no wind.

Navy regulations required that they be tested periodically lest you find yourself in a life raft with a Gibson Girl that didn't work. You had to be careful testing them, because when in proper use, they transmitted a series of evenly space tones that would set off alarms in every ship for hundreds if not thousands of miles. Bestowing upon you a kind of fame that you would not want.

We carefully avoided setting off these alarms while testing, by only using about six feet of antenna, and only powering up the Gibson Girl while inside the submarine, thus using the thick pressure hull to shield our test cry for help.

Once when I was a lowly Seaman, my Chief Radioman requested my assistance in testing our Gibson Girls. He did this by shouting, "Hawkins, get in here and crank this damn thing." The Radio Shack on a submarine is pretty small. It is about the size of the bathroom in most houses and it is full of radio equipment. This does not leave a lot of room for people. Inside the radio shack there were several radio receivers but only two speakers. The Navy however, provided us with a patch panel allowing us to connect any of the radios to either speaker. What my Chief did not know on this day, was that the speaker he was listening to for the signal from the Gibson Girl, was not patched to the radio that he was tuning. The stage was now set for my brush with death.

Crammed inside this tiny equipment filled room are my Chief and I and the Gibson Girl. I am sitting in "The" chair with the Gibson Girl strapped between my legs. My Chief is standing over me, next to the radio that he is going to use for the test. He has one hand on the radio tuning control and in the other hand he is carefully holding the short antenna wire by the insulated part. At his signal I start turning the crank. On the top of the Gibson Girl was a little light that would come on to tell you when you were cranking fast enough. I am cranking pretty fast and soon I see the light come on. I look up at my Chief as he is tuning the radio and we hear no sound from the speaker. After a minute he decides that the reason he is not hearing the signal is that I am not cranking fast enough. He politely urges me to increase me efforts by yelling at the top of his lungs, "Dammit Hawkins, put some elbow grease into that." Now I start really cranking hard and begin to work up a sweat, the light grows brighter. Still no sound comes from the speaker. This silence prompts my Chief to again urge me turn the crank faster by comparing my exertion to that of others by shouting, "Hawkins, my grandmother can crank it faster then that, get the lead out if you ever want to see daylight again." Thus motivated I begin turning the crank using both hands, my arms are a blur, sweat is flying everywhere, the light on the top is nearly blinding. The speaker is still silent. My Chief had just turned to recommend further efforts, when his finger slipped from the insulation on the antenna and touched the bare wire.

In an instant all of the electrons waiting impatiently to travel down the antenna suddenly found an easy path to ground right through my Chief. And at that same moment I am cranking as if my life depended on it.

Looking back I swear that there was a second or two when all of his hair stood straight out from his head. His leg muscles contracted and he leaped about 6 inches straight up. Unfortunately the light fixture in the overhead of the radio shack was only about two inches above his head. The resulting violent collision brought a shower of broken light fixture raining down on both of us. His body continued to jerk and twitch for a several seconds as I was still turning the crank for all I was worth. Then I stopped cranking as my body began to shake with laughter. That is when I was nearly killed.

The Sound of a Train
By Don Johnson, LT, USN (Ret) ex-RM1

The Peoria was by far the best and most fun duty station that I had. I was the Leading Petty Officer of CR Division (Communications-Radio) for pretty much of the 39 months I was onboard. It was my Radio Shack. In the eyes of my two chiefs, I could do no wrong.

I assigned all preventive maintenance (PMS—preventive maintenance system), created all inport and at sea watch bills and handled most of the training myself.

The Electronics Techs (ETs) or I conducted most corrective maintenance. I considered myself a pretty good technician, which caused problems with the ETs. They did not want a slimy "tweaker" to touch their equipment for repairs. We could operate it and break it, but don't touch it to repair it. It was their job.

Sometime in either 1977 or 1978, I can't recall the year, but we were having problems with a couple of transmitter patch panels. The knobs on the patch panels were not turning and setting correctly and it appeared to be slotted electronic wafers that were becoming degraded. The ETs wanted to wait until we pulled back into port and have the shore-based electronics people come aboard and fix it. I could not wait. I decided it was time for someone to take action.

I could not shut it all the way down because I had some operational circuits that needed to stay patched up on this particular patch panel.

I opened the patch panel to look at it again so that I could come up with a plan of action. I decided that if I zero out this particular knob that I would not bother anything else. The wafers appeared to be easy in replacing because once you zeroed that particular knob, the slots were all lined up and all you had to do was take a pair of needle nose pliers and pull the wafers out and then take the new wafers and push them back in. No problem.

I had a problem. The first couple of wafers at the top were easy taking out and replacing. But as I reached the bottom of this knob it got harder and harder. I was sitting in a chair with the patch panel open, the bottom was hinged, and it was lying on my lap. I had the brass cover also sitting in my lap. I was beginning to sweat a little because of the tediousness of this task. I was down to the very last wafer and as I was pushing this wafer in to seat it, the needle nose pliers slipped and slid to the back where they touched an electrical connection. I had a couple of guys sitting near me and they said that when those pliers hit the back of the patch panel, they thought they heard a train blowing its whistle, "Whoaoooa, Whoaoooa, Whoaooa!"

That electrical current shot up those pliers to my hand while the other hand was holding the brass cover. I screamed and I guess I was sounding like that Choo-Choo train that the guys thought they heard. The brass cover went flying and landed somewhere else in the Radio Shack.

I was always a stickler for safety. As I was getting myself back to normal, these two Radiomen were laughing at me. They said they had never heard such a good emulation of a freight train. I threatened both with bodily harm if they did not quit laughing. I was very serious. One of them, Ken Edmondson, told me that I should practice what I preach. I should have tagged and shut the power off to that patch panel if I was going to work on it. I shouted some kind of obscenity to him and walked out of the Radio Shack. I came back later to finish putting the last wafer in. This time, I tagged the power switch and turned the power off.

At the time, I didn't think the shocking surprise was funny. Now looking back, it was funny but I could have also died from electrical shock since that patch panel was operating off a 220v supply. For a few months after that those two called me Freight Train Johnson, a name that kind of stuck with me when I played poker.

Radio Shack Refresher Training
By Don Johnson, LT, USN (Ret) ex-RM1

This story isn't about a person being electrocuted or shocked but about some refresher training that our LST was going through one time off the coast of San Diego.

All ships go through REFTRA before deploying overseas. West coast ships go through it in San Diego and I guess most of the east coast ships go through it near Norfolk and down at Guantanamo Bay, Cuba.

One of the items they hit hard on in the training is safety and medical training such as cardio-pulmonary resuscitation (CPR).

Since our area had high voltage equipment the instructors were always having us go through some silly training exercise on shock victims and CPR.

I went through two refresher training exercises (REFTRA) while stationed on the Peoria. I always had a great group of guys working for me. All were very sharp and knew what they were doing once they were trained.

This particular REFTRA was a hard one. I had just reported back on board from teletype maintenance school and some of the guys were new and not well trained. Ken Edmondson was one of the experienced Radiomen in the shack and knew everything there was to know about it. However the training was somewhat lacking while I was away at school.

As we got underway for REFTRA, we were taking some major hits on some of the preliminary training. We were not doing so well.

Towards the end of the training we were beginning to pick up the pace and began passing the finals.

One of the finals consisted of treating an electrical shock victim.

The training observer grabbed an electronics technician by the name of Davy Jones (not real name) and had him lie on the deck in the transmitter room. Then he came out and told Ken Edmondson that there was a shock victim in the transmitter room and to come back to treat him.

Ken did go back. The observer asked him what would be the first thing that he would do. Ken said, "I would go get little Jimmy Sauers." And the observer said, "What?!"

Ken said, "I would go get little Jimmy Sauers."

And the observer said, "Now why would you go get little Jimmy Sauers?"

Ken said, "Because little Jimmy Sauers has never seen a dead man before."

You want to talk about fit to be tied. The observer came in and told me to get rid of Ken and get someone back there who was serious about training and if I did not get someone else back there in 60 seconds, he was going to fail us.

I was shocked that Ken didn't know what to do. Actually he did, but he was just trying to put a little humor into the training and the observer was in no mood for humor.

I got little Jimmy Sauers back there and he passed the final in treating a shock victim.

Even if Davy Jones had been a real shock victim, Davy probably would have died. He was one of those guys that you would not put your lips on his lips to save his life.

It is like the parable about the snakebite victim. The person who gets bit asks the other person to go get the first aid book and read about how to treat the snakebite. The book says you have to cut open the wound and suck the poison out. When the other person gets through reading the book, the snakebite victim asks what the book said. The other person says, "The book says you are going to die."

It was a lucky day for Davy since he was only a simulated electrical shock victim.

Joe Nearly Died
By Don Johnson, LT, USN (Ret) ex-RM1

The Guadalupe had just returned from a western Pacific (WestPac) deployment and doing our part on the line traveling the length of South Vietnam and up into the Gulf of Tonkin to refuel all of those ships.

I had just made RM3 and was very proud to be wearing the petty officer stripe with the eagle above the chevron which is sometimes called a crow.

We received new boot Radiomen onboard and one of them was Joe. I used to call Joe a bloodhound. He always had bags under his eyes like a bloodhound as though he never got a lot of sleep.

Not too long after he reported aboard he was placed in my watch section to train.

This was a small radio shack and not much to learn. The most difficult thing to learn was how to patch up radio circuits especially teletype circuits.

Just prior to making the WestPac, I was given the responsibility of doing preventive maintenance on the AN/SGC-1A, a teletype signal converter. One of the items I needed in order to complete the maintenance was a dummy plug to push into the teletype terminal connection. I made up my own dummy plug and then proceeded to open the cover to the terminal connector and as soon as I touched the connector with the dummy plug I was zapped with 60 milliamps of current. You want to talk about a shocking experience—that was one I did not want to re-live.

When it came time to train Joe, I was going to be sure that he understood that teletype equipment could be dangerous at any time regardless if you were setting up a live circuit or doing preventive maintenance. Teletype patch panels could be just as shocking if you inserted the patch cord into the wrong hole first. I tried to get this across to Joe. Either Joe was a little slow on the uptake or he did not care.

When I was training him on how to patch up a teletype circuit, I tried my best to teach him that you plug the patch cable into the looping jack first and not the set jack. I told him the set jack carried 60 milliamps of current and could shock you if you were not careful.

One of the patch panels was located above a message slot box that was made of stainless steel sheet metal. I was leaning on this box while instructing Joe on how to patch the circuit and something caught my attention and I turned my head. When I did, Joe plugged the patch cord into the set jack of the patch panel and when I noticed what he had done, I yelled at him and he dropped the other end of the patch cord on the stainless steel sheet metal slot box that I was leaning on.

It would be suffice to tell you that I once again received a shock. As I was pulling the patch cord out of the set jack I was screaming those four letter obscenities that most sailors use. Joe had already left the room. If he had not, I probably would have strangled him to death with one of the patch cords.

I called the Chief and asked him to put someone else in my watch section that could learn a little faster. He denied my request and I continued to try to train Joe to be a good radioman.

Joe eventually left the Navy as a conscientious objector and at one time had dated my sister. I do not know whatever happened to him, but on that particular day of training, Joe almost died (figuratively).

Chapter 5

<u>Great Navy Food</u>

Navy food has always been fairly good to the taste buds.

There are times when you wonder where the cooks got their training or even if they got any training at all.

I had seen many things done to Navy food that would make you reel and I have heard from former Filipino stewards about what some of them used to do to the food that they prepared for unpopular officers.

If you have a weak stomach, bypass this chapter. Some of the stories are quite humorous while others are just plain disgusting.

Irish Hobo's Bread
By Stephen Hawkins ex-RM2(SS)

I spent my time in the U.S. Navy in the 1960's as a Radioman on a fast attack submarine. Fast Attack submarines are those designed to find and sink other submarines. Mine was pretty cramped inside. There were a lot more people in the crew then there were bunks on the submarine. It has been compared to being shut inside a very small house in a third world country with a little over one hundred other people, for a couple of months at a time. Water is rationed, you share a bunk with someone in a different watch section, the sun never shines and you can never, ever go outside.

The navy did it's best to make our lives a little more livable by granting submarines a lot more money for food and by giving us excellent cooks to prepare it. The crew of my submarine enjoyed fresh baked bread and pastries every morning, steak and eggs for breakfast any day you wanted it. We really enjoyed every meal. This gastronomic heaven was only interrupted once, for two consecutive two-month patrols that seemed to last about a year.

We had several new shipmates report on board. Among them were a new cook and a new supply officer, both, I think, from some other planet. A deadly combination if there ever was one.

Our first indication that something might be amiss, was for years afterward referred to as "The day Poge almost died". To make Chipped Beef on Toast, also known as SOS, you are first supposed to soak the "chipped beef" in water over night to remove much of the salt. Not only did our new cook fail to do this, he added extra salt, and kept adding it until it tasted, to him, just right. The first of the crew to eat leaped up running for the corpsman after one bite. It was so salty almost none could stand it. There was one guy who did. A Machinist Mate named Poge became famous for eating a large plate full. We followed him around for days waiting for him to die.

You might want to make sure that children don't read this next part; it's just too disgusting. The Chipped Beef was followed in the coming days with an equally gruesome, "Peanut Butter Roast". There were other incidences, which occurred unfortunately with increasing frequency, for example, not knowing the difference between cloves, lots of them, and clove, one afternoon while making some sort of bizarre gravy. Have you ever tried to chew up several cloves?

The coup de grace, however was dealt when this particular cook and the new supply officer got together to order supplies for a two month patrol. They did not order enough flour. Consequently about half way through the patrol the fresh bread and pastries suddenly stopped. To say that the Captain and crew were not happy is an understatement. The Captain informed the cook and the supply officer that for the next patrol they would have enough flour if they had to sleep with it. He implied that if they failed to procure enough flour, the Navy might have its first keel hauling in years.

The next patrol we had flour. I mean there was flour stored everywhere. About 3 weeks out they ran out of yeast. At first they were afraid to tell the Captain. In what they thought was a clever ploy to avoid getting caught, they came up with something they called "Irish Hobo's Bread". It looked kind of like a huge doughnut placed on a plate in the middle of each table in the crews mess. By this time we were all a little gun shy, and so at first no one dared touch it. Finally the guy across from me, a large fierce man, known fleet wide for his courage, reached out tentatively with his knife to cut out a piece. From my vantage point I could see his face start to get red as he pushed down harder and harder with the sharp blade of the knife. This strenuous exercise had no visible affect on the large unmoving mass in the middle of the table. Next my shipmate gave it a solid rap with the handle of his knife. This produced a sound like one gets when whacking a cement block with a small hammer. Putting down his knife he picked up the "loaf" with his hands in an attempt to break off a piece. A good strong squeeze with his fingers dislodged only a few crumbs. Clutching the loaf in his right hand, he gave it a sharp crack on the surface of the table. This action dislodged a few more crumbs. I was one of the fortunate few who saw the look in his eyes and was able to quickly cover my head as he raised his arm and slammed the loaf down on the table with enough force to bring the Sonarmen running out of their sonar room. This produced a spectacular explosion of crumbs. The entire loaf disintegrated into millions of near microscopic pieces, which rained down on everyone in the crew's mess.

The rest of the patrol promised to be grim until somebody in the crew remembered how to get a sourdough starter going. We had fresh baked sourdough bread for the remainder of the patrol. The cook and the supply officer were transferred the minute we hit port. I am sure that this quick decisive action by the Navy contributed materially to bringing the cold war to an end much sooner then it would have otherwise.

Thousand Island Dressing and A Good Cup of Coffee
By Don Johnson, LT, USN (Ret), ex-RM1

While I was stationed aboard USS Independence, I had a Master Chief Radioman (RMCM) working for me who had formerly worked in wardrooms on small Navy ships as a steward. At one time in the Navy when Filipinos were recruited from the Philippines, they could only work in one rating in the Navy and that was the Steward (SD) rating. The SD rating disappeared in the mid-70s as a result of affirmative action.

Stewards were actually servants of the officers. They cleaned officer's quarters, did their laundry and cooked their meals. The rating was so closed up that they were lucky if they made SD2 in 20 years. Not too good for advancement purposes. It was very frustrating for them. Other frustrations came from having to work for unpopular officers; those who thought their stuff didn't stink.

The RMCM who worked for me on Indy told me a couple of stories about getting even with those unpopular officers. This is third hand so take it as you will.

RMCM told me that there was an officer onboard one of the ships that he served that was one of the most arrogant and most uncooperative individuals that he had ever served.

One day he said that he was going to get even with this officer. At lunch there would be a tossed salad with homemade Thousand Island dressing. As he was thinking about how he was going to get even it came to him to blow his nose into the Thousand Island dressing. The dressing had green relish in it anyway, so a little snot wouldn't matter. The officer would not be able to see it.

After the officers were served their salad and everyone put their favorite dressing on, the officer in question called RMCM over to his table. RMCM all of sudden had a guilty conscience and started to become scared. The officer then asked RMCM if he had made the Thousand Island dressing and when he said yes, the officer complimented him on such a tasty dressing. RMCM thanked him, walked out into the hallway and grinned to himself. Paybacks are hell. Did this officer get sick? RMCM said that he did not. What you don't know won't hurt.

Another ship and another situation for RMCM was that they had a wardroom full of arrogant officers.

What kind of payback was going to happen here?

RMCM said there was a steward who had the smelliest feet they ever smelled. He thought this guy's feet were affected by leprosy or something because they smelled so rotten.

One morning he and another SD grabbed this guy's smelly socks and went into the wardroom an hour before reveille and made coffee. They used those smelly socks as coffee filters.

He said he had never received as many compliments for the great coffee that morning. I don't know what was in the socks, but it must have added a nutty flavor to the Navy coffee that was stimulating to the palate.

For all of you arrogant officers out there, you had better be careful of how you treat your wardroom food and room attendants. You may get a surprise at lunch one day or a great cup of coffee some morning.

Pot Roast and Black-eyed Peas
By Don Johnson, LT, USN (Ret), ex-RM1

Back in the late 60's and early 70's while the Vietnam War was at its height, Navy ships got little time in their homeport. Sailors spent very little time with their families.

Prior to departing on a long deployment overseas, truckloads of frozen and dried food goods would be delivered pier side and it was not uncommon to hear a 100-man working party called away. I just happened to be a member of one of those 100-man working parties. We brought onboard hundreds of cases of soda, pasta, beans of all types, cases of frozen steaks and roasts, cigarettes, etc.

I noticed some of the cases of frozen steaks and roasts had dates stamped on them. This was 1970 and the dates stamped on the cases of meat were October 1943. Have you ever eaten twenty-seven year old beef, pork or turkey? Now who would really know unless you were looking for a date? The cooks knew.

The cooks knew because they knew this almost 30 year old meat had probably lost a lot of its texture and flavor and was freezer burned. During this particular deployment, we had Ginger Pot Roast, Spanish Pot Roast, Oven Pot Roast, English Pot Roast, Crappy Pot Roast, I'm Getting Tired of Pot Roast, you name it, we had some different type of pot roast two or three times a week. You couldn't tell if it was beef, pork or turkey. It all tasted the same, like dry leather with some flavoring.

That was nearly 30 years ago. I am now getting back into eating beef and pork pot roasts again, but also knowing that I have fresh meat to work with and not 30 year old frozen roasts.

Another time I was in the galley talking to one of my friends who was doing his time at mess cooking. All departments supplied so many sailors to help out in the mess decks to either clean or cook. This particular time while following my friend I stopped at a big vat that was cooking up black-eyed peas. I noticed little bugs floating on top of the boiling water. I asked what that was and he told me that they were boll weevils that had gotten in with the dried beans. He told me that it happens all the time and that all they do is scoop the dead weevils off the top and serve the peas anyway. He said the boiling water killed anything that they might have to cause illness.

I didn't eat any beans or black-eyed peas the remainder of the deployment and I told my other buddies to steer clear of those items, too.

Scrambled Eggs, "Got Milk?" and Fresh Baked Bread
By Don Johnson, LT, USN (Ret), ex-RM1

I have seen so many things over the years when it comes to food preparation. My father had been a short order cook for many years and finally retired after about 40 years as a cook. I never asked him if he had ever done anything to food for his customers. I don't want to know.

The story below is chronological in nature.

I had just completed recruit training in Great Lakes. The reporting date on my orders to Radioman "A" school was changed and I was to start at a later date, so they placed me in a holding company awaiting my transfer date.

This holding company acted as masters at arms for the restricted men's barracks. We were in charge of marching the restricted men to their assigned tasks.

One morning it was my duty to march the restricted men over to the galley to help prepare the food. Another holding company sailor and I were in charge of about a dozen restricted men.

When we got there, the cooks took them to their respective assignments and we were to walk around and keep tabs on them.

I went in the back to see what some of them were doing. One of the cooks had let about three of the restricted men loose to crack eggs and dump the yokes into a big vat for scrambling later. What I saw stunned me and made me somewhat sick to my stomach since all I ate for breakfast during the previous eight weeks or so was scrambled eggs.

The restricted guys were cracking the eggs, dumping the yoke in the vat and then spitting big hockers into the vat. I went back to get the head cook and told him what was going on and he told me that they did that all the time. He went on to say that saliva was not going to hurt anyone after it is cooked at a certain temperature. I then knew it was a lost cause.

I never ate scrambled eggs until much further into my career when I could watch them being made in front of my eyes. I normally ordered eggs to order such as over medium.

Just think. I had eaten those nasty scrambled eggs for breakfast for eight weeks.

Not too long after graduating from Radioman "A" school I was sent to USS Guadalupe.

Many people have to have milk everyday. I am one of those who doesn't really care for milk. I may have some with my cereal and that is about it.

Fresh milk is brought on board while in port. After being at sea for extended periods the milk runs out and powdered milk (yuck) takes its place.

On our way over to Vietnam we made a stop in Hawaii and we brought on fresh milk. About two days out I felt like eating a bowl of cereal. As I came through the chow line, I picked up a bowl and a couple of small packages of cereal. I got myself a glass of milk and poured it over the cereal. I did not think to smell the milk before I took a big spoonful of cereal and placed it in my mouth. I immediately spit everything back out. The milk was SOUR! I nearly vomited right then and there. Sour milk is the most disgusting thing you could put in your mouth. I found out later that what they thought was fresh milk was expired milk.

From then on, I never drank milk at sea.

Upon my return to active duty from 2 ½ years in the civilian world, the Navy sent me to USS Peoria, an LST. This was a ship renowned for its good cooks.

I knew why, too. The Chief cook was a short fat black man. He was as round as he was tall. He was the nicest guy, but loved to eat what he cooked.

There was another cook, a Petty Officer Second Class. He was the baker. He baked everything, bread, rolls, cakes, pies, you name it, he baked it. He was known for his fresh baked bread. I ate bunches of it.

One morning I was going to make some toast from the fresh bread that was made the night before. I got my eggs to order along with some sausage and hash browns. I grabbed about four slices of bread and was going to toast it. As I started pulling the bread slices apart to place in the rotating toaster I noticed something brown in the middle. I looked a little closer and guess what it was? It was a cockroach. Somehow a cockroach got into the bread batter and was cooked along with the bread. I didn't vomit or anything like that. I took the bread back to the cook and showed him what had happened. He told me not to tell anyone and went in and took the loaf that those slices came from and threw it away. He was very apologetic about it and did not want anyone to find out or it might hurt his reputation. I never did say anything to anyone about that incident.

I sure was careful about baked bread from then on.

I found out over the years that what you don't know isn't going to hurt you. Things that go on behind the closed doors of galleys stay a secret. If you knew what happened behind the doors of the galley of your ship, you would probably starve or hit the gedunk store and eat nothing but junk food.

I believe Navy cooks came up with Bill Clinton's military term long before he did; "Don't ask, don't tell."

Chapter 6

Hollywood Connections

There are times in our travels when we have all met celebrities, TV and movie stars, rock and roll artists, country western singers, and politicians. I had personally met three TV and movie stars while stationed aboard various ships.

You will read my three stories and then you will read some trivia at the end about a ship that has been used for different settings in movies.

Lloyd Bridges in Hong Kong
By Don Johnson, LT, USN (Ret), ex-RM1

We (the Guadalupe and crew) had just come off the line in Vietnam and were headed for some good R&R in Hong Kong. The date was around October or November 1970. It could have been late October or maybe early November. This would be my first time to Hong Kong and I was looking forward to shopping and getting drunk.

The first night in port was going to consist of a good steak and potato meal in a nice hotel and then do some drinking and hopefully dancing with other guests at the hotel. We chose the Hong Kong Hilton for dining, drinking and dancing. Sailors always like 3D entertainment.

We ate dinner at the HK Hilton restaurant and found out that drinking and dancing were available at The Den in the basement of the HK Hilton. After dinner we all decided to head to the basement to see what type of action was happening.

The Den was very dark; however, the drinks and music were great. We knocked down a few local beers and tried to get some of the hotel women guests to dance with us. When we thought that this place was really a dud, someone (I can't remember) asked if the person sitting across the dance floor was Lloyd Bridges. I don't remember who it was. However, everyone jumped on him and told him that Lloyd Bridges wouldn't be in this place. Then I started looking at this person sitting across the dance floor from us and it sure enough did look like Lloyd Bridges. I then started telling the guys that it was Lloyd Bridges. I asked who was brave enough to go over and ask. No one would. I then decided that I would go ask if he was Lloyd Bridges. I had enough booze in me that all of my inhibitions were gone.

I walked across the dance floor and introduced myself to him and it was Lloyd Bridges. He introduced me to his lovely wife (and to this day I can't remember her name) and to the then president and CEO of Capitol Records and his wife. I sat with them for a while and talked to them about what they were doing there and about what we sailors were doing in HK. I then asked him if it would be okay to bring my buddies over to meet him and his guests. He said sure. I believe there were about six of us total. I introduced all my buddies to Lloyd and his guests and he invited us to all sit down with them and have a few drinks and dance with his wife and the wife of the CEO.

We sat there until about midnight drinking and dancing. It was a lot of fun and we found out that Lloyd Bridges was a really nice guy and down to earth. He was there to shoot a new movie. I still can't remember the name.

He also cared about the guys who were still on the line or in country Vietnam fighting. Lloyd was patriotic.

I will never forget that one night in Hong Kong.

Heartbreak Ridge
By Don Johnson, LT, USN (Ret), ex-RM1

In late 1986, Belleau Wood was undergoing training and completing the Harrier op-eval for its first Harrier deployment overseas in 1987.

Belleau Wood at that time was the showboat of the Pacific Fleet. Everything happened on her. We hosted the California Women in Government Awards ceremony. SECNAV John Lehman dropped in via helo to see us. There were a multitude of other things that happened on board Belleau Wood after we came out of the yards in Bremerton.

The commanding officer (CO) took us into the yards and he brought us out on time. I began my Surface Warfare Officer (SWO) training under this CO. I began the SWO training only because I was passed over for LT the first time around due to a couple of adverse fitness reports (officer performance evaluations) I had received while stationed on Adak.

About the time the CO got us going, his time was up and another CO took command. Since I was the Assistant Communications Officer I saw every Naval message that came into the command.

When I first saw the messages coming in about Clint Eastwood and his filming a part of Heartbreak Ridge on Belleau Wood, I was excited. I was a Clint fan. I had seen every movie that he had ever made.

There was a rumor floating around that Clint and the CO were acquaintances and that is why Belleau Wood was selected.

The day of the movie shooting, they flew Clint's movie crew onboard to set up cameras, etc. The camera crew was trying to set up cameras in my radio transmitter antenna farm on top of the Signal Bridge and primary flight control. I told them that they could not set their equipment up in those areas unless they wanted to light up like Christmas trees. They relocated to a different location.

Later that day Clint flew onboard with other actors and they were all decked out in Marine camouflage and face paint. Our crewmembers were allowed to watch the filming.

Clint Eastwood

I had the 12:00-16:00 bridge watch as the conning officer. When they were through filming, Clint was escorted to the bridge to meet with the CO. Clint stayed and talked to him for a while and then was escorted back down to the flight deck to fly back off. On his way out he shook hands with a few of the crew including me.

I was in awe with Clint.

When the movie came out, I had to go see it since it had scenes filmed on Belleau Wood.

I felt great. I was the conning officer on Belleau Wood the day scenes from Heartbreak Ridge were filmed.

Quote from Heartbreak Ridge:

"It means be advised—that I'm mean, nasty, and tired. I eat concertina wire and piss napalm. And I can put a round through a flea's ass at 200 meters. So you go hump somebody else's leg mutt face before I push yours in!"

The Wonder Woman Connection
By Don Johnson, LT, USN (Ret), ex-RM1

Independence was a ship known for having movie stars on it. It was the ship that was used to film the shipboard scenes for **"The Flight of the Intruder"**. That was done just prior to my arrival. I found out that two of my people had bit parts in that movie. Scene remakes had to later be made on USS Ranger while we were over in the Persian Gulf.

When the movie came out after our return to San Diego, Indy officers and sailors were given a sneak preview the night before it hit the theaters.

During my two years on Indy, I had two commanding officers.

One was a screamer. I found out first hand about six weeks after reporting aboard. I tried to yell back but he stopped me and proceeded to continue the butt chewing. He later apologized while we had lunch together in his inport cabin. As far as I was concerned even after that episode and the apology, he was not flag material, but after all he was the Commanding Officer during the filming of **"The Flight of the Intruder."**

The other one on the other hand was one of those who could chew you out and you never knew you had been chewed out until after you left his cabin.

He was a smooth talker and I think he had some good connections in Washington, DC. He was flag material.

This CO also had friends on the West coast who had connections to Wonder Woman. That friend was Lyle Waggoner.

We had returned from Operation Desert Shield and had just completed a pier-side mini-overhaul so that we could travel from San Diego to Hawaii to relieve the Midway whose homeport was Yokosuka. The Midway was being retired.

On one of my duty weekends, I was the Officer of the Deck on a Saturday morning (0800-1200). The CO called down to the quarter-deck and told me that Lyle Waggoner would be showing up for a tour of the ship and to call him when Lyle and his family arrived and he would come down to the quarterdeck to take them on his nickel-dime tour.

I have never been a big fan of Lyle Waggoner and probably because he has never really played a leading role in anything. He had always played secondary and tertiary parts in movies, TV series and comedy shows.

Lynda Carter and Lyle Waggoner

He is probably best known for his secondary role in the TV series "**Wonder Woman**" with Linda Carter.

Around 11:00am I noticed a (I believe it was) Mercedes pull into the parking lot and Lyle Waggoner getting out. The rest of his family got out and came towards the ship. I called the CO and told him that Lyle Waggoner and family were on their way up the gangway.

Lyle and his family arrived at the quarterdeck before the CO, so I entertained them with a little knowledge of the quarterdeck and how it derived its name. By that time, the CO arrived to take them on a tour of the ship.

That was my short meeting with Lyle Waggoner and his family.

Many ships are seen in movies and sometimes you wander what ship that is. Here is a little trivia about USS Oriskany contributed by Larry Matthews.

Oriskany's Hollywood Connections
By Larry Matthews

THE BRIDGES AT TOKO RI: 1954. With William Holden, Grace Kelley, Fredrick March and Mickey Rooney—ALL CARRIER SCENES FILMED ABOARD THE ORISKANY.

TORA! TORA! TORA! 1970. With Martin Balsam, Jason Robards, Joseph Cotton, E.G. Marshall and James Whitmore—SCENES OF THE TAKE OFF OF JAPANESE AIRCRAFT ON THE MORNING OF THE ATTACK WERE FILMED ABOARD THE ORISKANY.

CAPRICORN ONE: 1978. Elliott Gould, James Brolin, Hal Holbrook, Karen Black, O.J. Simpson—A BRIEF MENTION AND VIEW OF THE ORISKANY AS THE PICKUP CARRIER OF THE SPACE CAPSULE.

MEN OF THE FIGHTING LADY: 1954. Van Johnson, Walter Pidgeon, Keenan Wynn, Frank Lovejoy—KOREAN WAR FILM SHOT ABOARD ORISKANY. Apparently the only ORISKANY-related film I have yet to see. Hope to remedy that situation.

USS FORRESTAL: SITUATION CRITICAL. 1999. John McCain and other FORRESTAL personnel are interviewed in this documentary of the USS FORRESTAL fire. THE ORISKANY IS SHOWN STEAMING TO THE AID OF FORRESTAL.

Chapter 7

Stories about Shipmates

Some of the stories in this chapter I can relate to and others I cannot. In **Utah Radiomen**, I cannot relate to because by the time I reported to my first ship and it sailed to Vietnam, we had already advanced past the Morse Code era into 60wpm and 100wpm teletype and cryptographic equipment. However, I was a Radioman and now that rating is gone. What we called Radiomen are now called Information Technology Specialists. They combined both the Radiomen and Data Processing Technicians into that rating.

You will read stories about other Navy radiomen.

There is a story from a World War Two veteran who served as a radarman on board USS Saratoga (CV-3) and as a tail gunner on a torpedo bomber.

How about reading something about women in the Navy? Sexual discrimination was a part of Navy life especially in an area where it should not have been.

Tragedy sometimes hits and you will read how two tragedies affected two sailors.

Utah Radiomen
By William Compton
Contributed by William Hughes

Most Navy Radiomen, from commencement of the wireless era down through both World Wars, Korea and possibly Vietnam, stood "split phone" watches. Sometimes they would monitor a Navy operating frequency in one ear, and listen for distress calls from the International Distress Frequency of 500 Kilocycles (now called Megahertz), in the other ear.

USS Utah (BB-31) before Pearl Harbor

An innovative Radioman standing a single frequency watch learned to "split phones" with radio stations—local if near land, or "short wave" at sea. This was generally frowned on by management; i.e., the Chief Radioman, who would raise h——if he found out about it. But radio watches on most ships were long—Midnight to breakfast, breakfast to 1600 (4PM), and 1600 to 2400 (Midnight). The midnight to breakfast was known as the "mid watch" and was the most relaxed for the operators. Thus it was not unusual to be copying code through one ear and listening to Benny Goodman, Guy Lombardo, Glenn Miller, or some other great "Big Band" through the other ear.

You may be thinking that using "dots and dashes" to spell out the alphabet, send numbers and punctuation was a slow and cumbersome way to communicate. However, many a Navy RM could copy Morse code at 60 words per minute, drink a cup of "Joe" and carry on a conversation at the same time.

Today, the military, government, and commerce use voice and data communications, transmitting via satellite systems, microwave and fiber optics. The Internet has rapidly replaced many of the "horse and buggy" communication systems and is providing the most effective communications seen by this "communicator" of sixty years.

There is one holdout group still using International Morse Code—some Amateur Radio Operators who still value the reliability of this "archaic" form of communications aka "CW."

So as you listen to music and International Morse Code, imagine you are a Navy Radioman on a long cruise across the ocean of your choice. You are on the "mid watch" and from topside moonlit water can be seen in all directions. *Oh yes, there's not a woman in a thousand miles! (see disclaimer)*

Disclaimer: This page was written in reminiscence of a bygone era. It is not meant to discredit in any way, the great contribution of women to communications, military operations, computers, or anything else.

Eyewitness Report
By William (Bill) Hughes, Rm3/c USN

I had been aboard the USS Utah for more than a year. I had learned my way around that huge ship during the first few months aboard as a radio messenger.

HUGHES, William E. Rm3/c
1940-41 (1945 Photo)

It is true that I was a *lost* a great deal of the time. Prior to December 7th I had been promoted from sleeping on a hammock with one of the Deck Divisions to the more luxurious "radio operator" bunk room adjacent to Main Radio where we slept on cots. We were located two decks below the main deck, and one deck above the engine room.

Life aboard the Utah had been great. I had made the transition from farm boy to the rating of Radioman, third class, and had come to enjoy the cohesiveness of my fellow radio operators. The operations of the Utah as a bombing target, an AA machine gun school, a submarine target and radio controlled ship was carried out in a disciplined manner; however, our lifestyle was comparatively relaxed. The "chow" was excellent and there was more liberty than we "grunts" could afford.

But at 07:55 AM, Sunday Morning, December 7th 1941, our lives would be changed forever. We had not been trained to anticipate a major, all out *sneak attack* by a large force of foreign military aircraft from a country with who we were not at war.

On that lazy Sunday morning, most off-duty radiomen were asleep on our dry comfortable cots in the bunk room. The tumultuous explosion that rocked the ship almost threw us out of our bunks. We must have been looking at each other in sheer amazement. One man, Radioman 3/c Warren Upton was dressed and "spiffed up" for a day ashore. He was bending over someone's cot attempting to obtain an object from his locker. Another said we had been rammed [by another ship].

Within 20 or so seconds, a second jarring explosion again rocked the ship, also from the port side, and within minutes the USS Utah was taking on a pronounced list to port. It was obvious to all of us that we needed to reach the top side immediately. As I recall, our departure from the sleeping quarters was orderly but swift. Up two ladders and we found ourselves huddling under a protected part of the superstructure called the starboard air castle.

By this time, Jap aircraft were making strafing runs on the hapless sailors who were exposed to their fire. Since all our guns had been covered for bombing practice the week before, we could not fire back, and the giant ship was listing rapidly to port. Personnel who came up from below and entered the deck on the port side were in immediate danger of being crushed from falling timbers, and many were. These timbers protected our deck and provided a viable target for practice bomb hits to be marked when we were participating in bombing exercises.

It has been stated that an order to "Abandon Ship" was given. I failed to hear the command above the noise and bedlam. It became a matter of every man for himself. Personally, I felt an urgent need to distance myself from the ship, and a leap over the starboard side fairly early in the game found me swimming to the mooring quay where I was able to hide behind the pilings during the continuing strafing runs.

A great danger faced by all of us was jumping on someone or debris in the water, or being jumped on by someone else. Fortunately I was spared from this hazard.

At the first lull in activity, I swam for shore, and the only scratch I received during World War 2 occurred when wading up the beach onto Ford Island. I cut my bare foot on a piece of coral. It was minor; it did not delay me from seeking refuge in the pipe line ditch where most of the crew ended up until the planes of our "newly acquired enemy" finally returned to their carriers. There, I "hunkered down" dripping wet in my "skivvy" shirt, shorts and a pair of white knee high tropical trousers. All my personal belongings, including a prized photo of movie actress Rita Hayworth, remained aboard ship in my locker.

While hunkered down in the ditch, watching terror reign from the skies, these thoughts: (1) Where in the h—are all these planes coming from and how long will they keep coming, and (2) I asked my nearby shipmates "what do you think "Washington" is going to say about this?" The latter expression stemmed from the fact that I was being trained to copy wireless press news for the ship. For weeks there had been numerous and lengthy press releases datelined "WASHINGTON" with announcements and comments on the world situation.

We observed some fine moments. First and foremost was the heroic action of Warrant Officer Stanley Symanski and the men from the USS Raleigh and Utah, who volunteered to go back aboard the big broad bottom of the now capsized Utah in the face of enemy fire, and cut our Shipmate Jack Vaessen out of the double bottoms. It is gratifying to know that some 61 years later Jack is alive and living in California. So is Warrant Officer Symanski, who retired from the Navy as a Commander. Other personnel exemplified unusual valor in disregarding their safety and operating small boats to ferry personnel from the doomed ship to shore. Others lent a hand to wounded shipmates in distress. It was our worst hour and yet our finest hour.

In the lull between the two attacks many of us moved out of the ditch and took shelter in a building on Ford Island. During the second part of the attack we simply took shelter in a metal building and hoped to heck they missed our building. As there were no windows in the building, I assume we were in some kind of storage building, and our inability to observe what was going on outside was scary.

As is eloquently told in the EW reports of Warren Upton and others, most of us ended up aboard the USS Argonne, our Base Force Flag Ship for the night of December 7th. As the boat carrying us from Ford Island made it's way across the Harbor to what was known as "1010 docks," we observed the terrible site of the mangled superstructure of the USS Arizona, the capsized Oklahoma, the sunken California, Nevada, Maryland and other ships, such as the destroyers, Downs and Cassin, and Shaw, the latter three being almost obliterated in Dry-dock. These sights gave us a knot in the pit of our stomachs and very heavy hearts.

On the night of December 7th, we brought up ammunition which has been stored in the "bowels" of the Argonne, something new to the manicured nails of a radioman. It would get worse, as we would go back on December 8th and retrieve ammo from inside the Utah, where welders had cut entrances into the bottom.

We were the lucky ones, collecting ammunition; many were assigned the job of collecting bodies and body parts from the murky waters of the harbor. Many remains would be buried in unmarked graves. We later learned that most of them were from the USS Arizona and Oklahoma; apparently, some of them were from the Utah and efforts are ongoing now to identify them. An excellent story on this topic appeared in the November 5th 2001 edition of the Honolulu Advertiser.

While aboard the Argonne the night of December 7th, one more shipmate from the Utah, Pallas Brown, Seaman 2nd class would die from a stray bullet fired by nervous gun crews (some say from the USS California,) who were shooting at what they thought were enemy planes returning in another Jap. Unfortunately, they were firing on inbound aircraft from the USS Enterprise which had been given clearance to land on Ford Island, causing a tragic loss of more American lives. Shipmate Palace Brown, as well as some of the Enterprise's pilots may well have been the first casualties from "friendly fire" during the United States role in World War II. Seaman Leonard Price of the USS Utah was wounded at the time Shipmate Brown was killed. Leonard Price recovered, and I am happy to report that as of Sept. 1, 2002 Leonard is still living.

I spent one week aboard the USS Vireo, a mine sweeper, as a temporary replacement for their Radioman who was in the Hospital. On December 15th, I was transferred to the USS Saratoga, an Aircraft Carrier, (CV3) which was destined to be torpedoed on January 11, but fortunately not sunk. I would serve on other ships being newly commissioned and hurriedly sent to the Pacific where the war was not going well for the U.S. until after the Battle of Midway.

The long trek from Pearl Harbor to Tokyo Bay lasted 3 years, 8 months and 25 days. I can truthfully state that I was where it started the day it started, and where it ended the day it ended—although my ship, the USS Gasconade (APA85,) an Attack Transport, did not drop anchor in Tokyo Bay until 11:00 on Sept. 2, 1945. Alas, the surrender ceremony was over and Navy records do not show Gasconade as being present when the surrender was signed. That long trip was paid for by many

American lives as well as lives of our Allies and the Japanese. It is said that the military is only needed when the diplomats fail. Let's hope we keep America militarily strong, the diplomats do not fail and this terrible history will never be repeated.

Old Sailors
By Anonymous

Contributed by Don Johnson

We old sailors sit and chew the fat
'bout how things used to be
of the things I've seen
and places I've been
When I ventured out to sea.

I remember friends from long ago
and the times I had back then
of the money I've spilled
and the beer I've swilled
In the days with my sailing friends.

Our lives are lived in days gone by
with thoughts that forever last
of cracker-jack hats
and bell-bottom blues
and the good times in my past.

I recall long nights with a moon so bright
far out on a lonely sea
and the thoughts I had
as a youthful lad
When our lives were unbridled and free.

I know so well how our hearts would swell
when the flag fluttered proud and free
and the stars and the stripes

made such beautiful sights
as we plowed through an angry sea.

I talk of the bread ole' cookie would bake
and the shrill of the boatswain's pipe
and how the salt spray fell
like sparks out of hell
when a storm struck in the night.

I remember mates already gone
who forever hold a spot
In the stories of old
when sailors were bold
and lubbers were a pitiful lot.

We sailed our ship through many a storm
when the sea was showing its might
And the mighty waves
might be digging our graves
as we sailed on through the cold black night.

I speak of nights in a bawdy house
somewhere on a foreign shore
and the beer we'd down
as they gathered around
while cracking jokes with a busty whore.

My sailing days are gone away
never more will I cross the brow
But I have no regrets

for I know I've been blessed
'cause I have honored the sacred vow.

Our numbers grow less with each passing day
as our chits in this life are called in
But we've nothing to lose
for we've all paid the dues
and we'll sail with our shipmates once again.

I've heard them say before getting underway
that there's still some sailin' to do
and I'll exclaim with a grin
that my ship has come in
and the Lord is commanding the crew.

I've been wanting to pen these thoughts
since learning to tie my first knots
for it's the love of these memories for me
that makes me yearn for the sea

I've laid down the pen for now
and bask in these memories
I tip my glass to all former shipmates
and wish them following seas.

Navy Radiomen on the USS Sanctuary (AH-17)
By Butch Weghorst

The following are some of my experiences while aboard USS Sanctuary from November 1966 to March 1968.

When we first began duty on the ship following Pre-Com School in Norfolk, there were only about 7 of us. A petty officer first class, a second class, a third class, the rest were Radioman Seamen (RMSN). We had a LT Communications officer and his assistant was an ensign. While underway, we worked port & starboard watches (12 on, 12 off) and 3 guys to a watch. Usually breakfast to supper, supper to breakfast. The first class only worked days in his office in radio central.

The workload was generally light between New Orleans and the west coast. When we finally got to Vietnam in April of 67, we really got busy. During this period of time, US Navy hospital ships were not allowed to use crypto or other "covered" circuits. Something to do with the Geneva Convention.

Our primary method of sending and receiving traffic was via CW (Morse Code). We used voice with some of the other ships and commands when in the war zone. We took care of sending and receiving all ships' company traffic as well as all hospital company traffic. We all became experts at sending and receiving code with average sending/receiving speeds of 18-22 words per minute.

Each day, we sent out hundreds of messages, most of it being hospital traffic. Patient status reports and death reports were sent out daily. I can remember sending a patient status report on an Army Sgt named Carter every day for 5 weeks before he died. After a while, you would get to feel you knew the person. If any of you are familiar with Navy milstrip supply requisitions, we sent those out as well. These were very long complicated messages used to order supplies. They contained mostly federal stock numbers with a lot of numbers and symbols. Since we were unable to send and receive classified traffic, it was sent out and brought in by messenger. In Danang, one of us radiomen would go ashore when a boat was going in and take our outgoing classified stuff to Navsuppact Danang and pick up whatever they had for us. In Subic Bay, we relied upon other ships or the local Navcommsta to help us out. In Hong Kong and Singapore, we relied upon the designated SOPA (Senior Officer Present Afloat) ship to do this for us.

USS Sanctuary off the coast of Vietnam

When in port, in order for all radiomen to get time off, our entire message guard was usually handed over to a SOPA ship or Navcommsta (Naval Communications Station). Each morning, we would take outgoing and pick up incoming traffic, distribute it, then hit the beach.

When in Subic Bay, most all the radiomen on the Sanctuary hung out at the Oriental Bar in Olongapo City.

As you probably know, the Sanctuary spent a lot of time at sea. After about 6 months of this 12 on and 12 off routine, most of us RM's were fairly "batty" from Morse Code going through our heads every day, day after day. I still hear it to this day and will never forget it.

After about 6 months of being on station most of the time, we were able to establish an unclassified Teletype net with Navcommsta, San Miguel in the Philippines (NPO) (NPO was the call sign for that station). This worked very well and took a good deal of pressure off us. By this time, we had all made rate and a few new faces had arrived to help out.

On the Sanctuary, auxiliary radio (or back-up radio) was known as "Radio 3". It was seldom used for official Navy communications. The ship ordered Collins ham radio gear, the radiomen and the one and only ET we had installed it in Radio 3, and the ship got a ham radio station license from the FCC. During off time, the ET and radiomen volunteered to make calls to ham operators in the states so the patients and crew could call home via phone patches. We would post a list on the door, callers would sign it, and it would be first come, first served. Patients were usually given priority of the first session. The ship's company and hospital company the second session. This was usually done in the evenings during the week and most anytime on weekends. This was a great moral booster.

The night shift in radio (supper to breakfast) would usually have all traffic sent by midnight. We would then "field day" radio central. After that, we would have nothing much to do except scan receiving frequencies on the upper AM band and find the Hanoi Hanna program. We would then tune up one of our large WRT-1 Westinghouse transmitters on radio teletype tones at 1 kilowatt output and jam the frequency by transmitting a continual ""test tape". Before long, the Gooks would change frequencies. We would then scan up and down the AM band until we found them and then jam the hell out of them again. This could go on for hours. We had to find something to do to amuse ourselves. Of course, none of our superiors (officers) ever knew.

Sara Stories
By Vern Bluhm

During WW II I served on an aircraft carrier, the USS Saratoga (CV3). The following is a couple of incidents that happened while I was aboard her.

A young Ensign, just out of flight school, came aboard and started throwing his weight around big time. Not one of the flight deck crew liked him and it was to the point that it was unsafe for him to walk on flight deck alone on dark nights. The Chief of the Flight Deck one day took this young Ensign aside and told him; "Sir, it is not my place to tell you how to be an officer, but I would like to remind you of one thing. These men on the flight deck have to get you off the flight deck but they do not have to get you back on it." The message got through to the pilot loud and clear; overnight he made a complete turnaround.

The second incident occurred during the battle for Iwo Jima. The Sara was in support of the Marines on the island when the Japanese attacked us. During the attack we received three bomb hits and three kamikaze hits. Our first hits were on our catapults. During one of the lulls in the attack a plane from one of the other carriers kept indicating that he wanted to come aboard, so we landed him. The Landing Signal Officer (LSO) walked to the plane after it came to stop and the pilot jumped out of the plane and told the LSO, "You should be glad that you are not on the Sara. She is getting the hell kicked out her." When the LSO told the pilot that he was on the Sara, he fainted.

Combat Action Ribbon
Authorization to wear with uniform effective
December 7, 1941

His Watch
By Theresa Davis

At attention, his senses on alert, he watches into the night.
Gun at side, eyes opened wide.
He chose this life, decided his believes were worth the fight.
So, here he stands over the water, as in moves the tide.

No fear he possesses.
He has brothers there to protect him.
But tonight is his turn, his turn to repay the awareness.
So, he stands there, with his brothers' trust in him.

Hours pass, as his watch grows to an end.
The sun appears over the horizon,
along with the sleepy eyes of his brothers.
He was there with a helping hand to lend.
Now, he turns over his watch, puts his trust in one of his many brothers.

The Times and Life of a Woman In The Navy
By Yuvonne Wolfe

I was born in Callender, Iowa on 20 May 1933, But my life really began on a fateful day in late April, 1954. I had been working in the credit department of a large Topeka, KS furniture and appliance store since shortly after I graduated from Hiawatha (KS) High School in May, 1951. This particular day, my supervisor and I had a disagreement about how to deal with shortages in a cash drawer, mine in particular, to which anyone and everyone in the office had access. He angrily told me I was fired. Equally angry, I told him he couldn't fire me and that I had just quit! I stormed out of the office and left the store. I had made a life-altering decision that was going to launch me into a new and exciting life and career. Of course, I didn't know it then.

I walked about two blocks down the street and into the United States Post Office. Unhesitatingly, I went straight to the United States Navy Recruiting Office. "Sign me up!" I demanded. The recruiter was happy enough to do so, but informed me I would need the written permission of at least one parent since I wasn't 21. On the way home that evening, I told Dad about my sudden unemployment and of my decision to join the Navy. I told him that either he or Mom would have to sign for me. After discussing it with Mom, he reluctantly agreed to sign. A day or two later Dad signed, I signed, and I was on my way. There was no looking back now.

My next stop was Kansas City, MO. The Topeka recruiter put me on a Greyhound bus for the trip to Kansas City. Someone from the Kansas City recruiting office met me at the bus terminal and checked me into a room in a downtown hotel. I hardly slept a wink that night. I was both scared and excited. The next morning, the recruiting office sent someone to escort me to their offices where I was interviewed to be sure I was in my right mind. I signed more papers, was given a physical and pronounced fit for duty, was given my Navy serial number and then sworn in by a woman naval officer. It was 3 May 1954.

After my swearing in, I was given a sealed envelope containing my orders, a train ticket, and then taken to Union Station and put on a train bound for the U.S. Navy Recruit Training Command, Bainbridge, Maryland. I soon found a comrade. I recognized a young man who had just re-enlisted at Kansas City and who was on that train and also bound for Bainbridge. I quickly made friends with him and we "hung out" during our trip.

Arriving in Bainbridge, I was met by someone from the Recruit Training Command. I was soon at the training command and was stripped of my civilian clothing, fitted for "granny" shoes, given several pair of long, cotton hose, supplied with a variety of uniforms and given a bad haircut. Suddenly, there I was, transformed, standing tall and proud in a brand new, navy blue uniform with shiny gold-colored buttons, and wearing cotton stockings and granny shoes! I was in the Navy and never felt prouder of myself than I did at that moment!

I graduated from boot camp in July and was assigned to another training command. My orders read "For duty under instruction," at the Communications Technician School, Naval Security Group Activity, Imperial Beach, CA. I was destined to become a CTO (Operations Branch). The Operations Branch involved work in cryptography, communications security, teletype operation, and use of the International Morse Code. I would be working with highly classified information and required an equally high security clearance. To qualify for the security clearance, my background was thoroughly checked by the FBI to ensure I would be worthy of being given access to this sensitive information. Nothing derogatory turned up in the investigation (I knew it wouldn't...I didn't know how to get into trouble then) and I was granted a Top Secret security clearance.

I arrived at the Imperial Beach CT School in August 1954 and completed my training in March 1955. I was transferred to my first duty station. My orders read: Transfer to Naval Security Group Command, Washington, D.C. for duty with National Security Agency, Arlington Hall Station, Arlington, VA. When I arrived in Washington, I was in awe of my surroundings! Arlington, VA is directly across the Potomac River from Washington, D.C. My barracks sat on a big hill looking down on the Pentagon! Every time we rode a city bus to D.C. we passed through the Pentagon! Arlington National Cemetery was next door to the barracks! I could see many of the federal buildings and the dome of the capital building in D.C.! I admit I was awed and impressed when I saw the Pacific Ocean for the first time, but the sight of these buildings took the cake. I had seen pictures of them in my history books, but suddenly, here I was, gazing on them in person! I can still see the views in my mind's eye.

When I reported for duty at Arlington Hall Station I was a seaman striker, meaning I was to continue my training on-the-job, then I would be tested and, if I had learned well, I would become a Communications Technician 3rd class, Operations Branch. I passed this test with flying colors. I sewed on my CTO3 "crow" with great enthusiasm! I was looking forward to the increase in pay!

Arlington Hall Station was an Army post. I was assigned to work in the National Security Agency's Telecommunications Department (T/COMM). T/COMM was a huge place, encompassing one entire wing of a temporary wooden building built as an Army barracks during WWII. All of its many windows had been nailed shut and all the glass in them had been painted over. Security was obviously paramount. The floors were bare wood with dust so deeply engrained that one could never entirely sweep them clean. Believe me, many had tried! The place was wall-to-wall, noisy cryptographic equipment and chattering teletypes, tape reperforators and other communications equipment, much of which I had never seen. I was soon to be on very intimate terms with all of it. One had to shout to be heard over the roar of the equipment. To this day, I am unable to hear certain pitches of sound due to the abuse my hearing suffered from nearly three years of working with all that equipment.

In the fall of 1957, The National Security Agency moved its operations from Arlington Hall Station to a new building at Ft. Meade, Maryland. All female U.S. Navy personnel were transferred to the Naval Security Station, Washington, D.C. I was assigned to the Communications Department for the few months remaining on my enlistment, which was up in May 1958. The economy in 1958 was poor and jobs were scarce, so I decided to reenlist early and for six years in March 1958. I was immediately transferred to the Naval Security Group Activity, Wahiawa, HI, for a two-year tour. I was among the privileged few to participate in Hawaii's glorious statehood celebration in 1959.

In March, 1960 I was transferred back to the Naval Security Group Command, Washington, D.C. I had switched my specialty from Operations to Administrative and had been promoted to CTA1. (Translated: Communications Technician, Administrative, First Class or E-6) I took my discharge in March, 1964 and returned to the same office three weeks later as a civilian, GS-7 doing the same work I had been doing before I was discharged. My intention to become a "lifer" had been sabotaged when the Navy determined it no longer needed or wanted women in the CT ratings. I wanted to continue doing the work I had come to enjoy. Taking my discharge and accepting civilian employment with the Naval Security Group was the only way I could continue my career.

With the exception of about two years between September 1966 and June 1968 when I decided I should give the "true civilian world" a try (bad decision!), I continued with my career in the world of cryptography and communications security. I retired as a civilian, GS-12, on 3 June 1988. If I had it all to do over again, I wouldn't change one thing!

The Tragedy of Peter Chan
By Larry Matthews

I never met, nor to my knowledge, did I ever see Peter Chan. However, the circumstances of his death and the coincidence which occurred later have left an indelible memory in my mind.

September 25, 1972 was a typical day aboard the American Aircraft Carrier ORISKANY. We were off the coast of Vietnam launching air strikes at the North Vietnamese. Along with us were two destroyer escorts.

I had only been aboard the ORISKANY for about a month. I had flown to the Philippines in early August and had been assigned to the Captain's Office, as part of X Division. The year before I had been assigned to an Ammunition Ship, the USS MAUNA KEA and had spent four months, in the combat zone off of North Vietnam. Aboard MAUNA KEA I had been assigned to 3rd Division.

Peter Chan was a Seaman Apprentice in Third Division. He was a fellow Californian, as he had grown up in San Francisco. He was 20 years old. There is a rule aboard U.S. Navy ships that, when trash is thrown overboard, the sailor takes the trash to the back end of the ship, known as the "fantail" and properly throws it off. The breaking of this rule was to start a chain of events that was to lead to the death of Peter Chan.

As far as I know there was never any determination of who threw the trash off the side of the carrier. But the trash was thrown and some of it was blown back and hit Peter Chan. Peter saw who dumped the garbage and ran after him.

At the time, Peter and the trash thrower were located in an area just below the flight deck known as the "hangar bay". It is the place where the planes are brought down by elevator from the flight deck so they can be repaired and maintained. Another section of the ORISKANY hangar bay was the scene of a horrible fire in October of 1966 which resulted in the deaths of 44 sailors.

When maintenance tests are performed, a jet's tail is turned toward the outside—or ocean side—of the hangar bay so that when the engine is turned on for testing the jet flame can do no damage to the ship. There is usually a space of several feet between the end of the engine and the edge of the deck.

The following events are hearsay to me but I believe they are fundamentally true. When Peter took off after the man who threw the trash, the man ran in front of a jet fighter that had its engine turned on for testing. Peter, for some reason, ran behind the jet.

The jet's engine blew Peter Chan off of the carrier into the Tonkin Gulf. A fall from the hangar bay to the sea is a long one, but it can be survivable.

I was in the Captain's Office when I heard the "man overboard" emergency call over the 1MC, or ship's loudspeaker system. When this occurs, the ship immediately does a "180"—complete turn around to get back to the original place where the man went overboard.

Additionally, the two destroyer escorts make immediate headway toward the area.

I understand that someone on the destroyers saw Peter in the water and saw him wave. But then he disappeared.

It was never determined what happened to him in the water. Sharks often follow Navy Ships. Possibly the blast of the jet engine was just too much for him. Or possibly the fall may have been fatal.

We had a memorial ceremony for Peter. A sailor from my office, Ronnie McFarland, sang. Ronnie was previously one of the Edwin Hawkins Singers and did a wonderful job.

In December of that year, just before Christmas, I was in Subic Bay, a major naval base in the Philippines. It was during the time of the Christmas Bombing that eventually led to the North Vietnamese signing the peace treaty the next month.

I was at the Sampaguita Club on base when I ran into friend of mine from the USS MAUNA KEA. His name was Michael, and he and I had served together for seven months the previous year. We decided to have a few drinks together and talk over old times.

Later in the evening, Michael indicated to me that he had a friend aboard ORISKANY with whom he had grown up with in San Francisco. Did I know a Peter Chan?

It is still inconceivable to me that, of the 3,500 sailors stationed aboard the ORISKANY, that the one man Michael grew up with—and asked me about—was the one and only man who was killed during the entire time I served aboard the ship. And I had to be the one to tell my former shipmate that his lifelong friend was dead.

Peter Chan's name appears on both the national Vietnam Veteran's Memorial in Washington D.C. and the California Vietnam Veteran's Memorial in Sacramento. It also remains in my mind as a reminder of how fragile life is—and how little time we really have on earth.

(I want to thank Daniel Delaney and John Castelvetro for their input in April 2000. They also were both aboard ORISKANY that day and they knew Peter Chan. They helped correct a few errors and misunderstandings that appeared in the original story. Thanks guys!)

In Memory of Lt. Roy Hubert Hodge III
By ABH2 Dave Foley

The drowning accident of Lt. Hodge on the 30th of July 1982, from the deck of the Carrier USS Independence CV-62 has been relived in my mind thousands of times. It is one reason why I suffer from PTSD.

This may not have been a case of Pilot error as so many of us were told. The EA6-B this crew was flying in parted an arresting gear wire. The Planes arresting gear hook did not fully engage the wire. I've been told it was embedded in the cable about one quarter of the way. Actually cutting the cable itself, in a normal trap the hook captures the wire. (Picture your hand around an ice cream cone.) The plane was not at full power after the trap and may have come to a complete stop, when this small section of cable parted.

The Bird slowly rolled off the angle deck and into the water. The flight crew ejected before the bird rolled off the deck and hit the sea. There was a panicked concern that only three chutes were seen, word was quickly received and put out that one of the back seats had been flown empty. Two of the aviators in fully deployed chutes drifted clear of the slowly sinking plane. They were watched from the point of their ejection until they were picked up by rescue helos from the Independence.

Lt. Hodge was not to be that fortunate. His chute did not appear to have fully opened and if it did it was to close to the sea to make a difference. Lt. Hodge landed on top of the now crippled and sinking plane his chute enveloping both himself and the slowly sinking aircraft.

From both the Flight Deck and the Hanger Bay, helpless crew members watched in shocked horror. I remember throwing my P.F.D. along with many other crew members into the water. The water around the stricken aircraft was littered with any items that would float. Both the 5 and 3 MC's blasted orders that no one was to jump into the water. I don't recall the crash alarm being sounded, I'm told it was. I remember no noise other than the 5mc. The ship had commenced a slow turn returning to the site of the accident and went D.I.W. (dead in the water).

I and others watched as Lt. Hodge tried in vain to free himself from the chute that may have saved him otherwise.

After what seemed like hours, the chute entangled with the Prowler slowly sunk and took with it LT. Roy Hubert Hodge III.

This year (July 2001) while talking to some coworkers, my conversation about this accident was over heard by a third party.

This person angrily asked me where I heard this story. I told him in no uncertain terms that I didn't hear the story, I lived it! He recounted that he had been a bar tender and heard a story very much like the one I've told above.

There's only one shipmate I've run into from the area I use to call home. I told this man that I had run into a shipmate about 1987-88, tall skinny, dirty blond haired guy. The third party said this was the guy. He was visibly shaken, seems for all these years he never knew if this story was true or not. I have confirmed it for him. He told me the next day he couldn't sleep now knowing that this was a true story, I told him he only lost one nights sleep, I've got him well beat!

Please also remember that this is how I relive the story in my own mind. It does not match the official version I'm sure.

Others I've talked to recall the accident almost the same way.

One shipmate was watching the event directly below were I was standing on the flight deck, he was in the hanger bay. I never met Lt. Hodge, I am sure like the rest of the Men of VAQ-131 he was great guy. I know I'll never forget this man, I only hope to see him while I'm on my final cruise.

Chapter 8

Drunken Sailors, Fighting Sailors

At one time in the Navy, it was expected of sailors to go out and get drunk and to get into fights.

You will read true stories about drunken sailors and fighting sailors or even drunken fighting sailors.

In the mid-1980's the Navy began to de-glamorize the use of alcohol because of state drunk driving laws. Many a good sailor began to feel the arm of the law when they had to answer to both the civilian law and the UCMJ for the same offense.

Lou Stoumen
Drunken Sailors, Times Square
1940

If you were convicted of drunk driving off the base, the civilian authorities would send information to the base or ship CO. Then the UCMJ would get you normally on some type of "unbecoming" article and an additional fine.

If that didn't get your attention, then you probably did have a drinking problem and were pushed into one of the Navy's alcohol rehabilitation programs.

Sit back and read about those drunken fighting sailors.

The Fighting P-Boat
By Don Johnson, LT, USN (Ret), ex-RM1

In an earlier story I talked about USS Peoria and the "perfect storm". Well this ship on that particular WestPac cruise or deployment had other things going on. She had a crew that loved to fight and not amongst themselves but with other ships' crews.

We fought in every port we pulled into.

At the Enlisted Men's (EM) club in Pearl Harbor, many of the P-boat's crewmembers set up several tables together to show our unity.

Other ships' crews began doing the same thing. Now all of a sudden you have a problem. The "our ship is better than your ship" syndrome took affect.

I had the duty the first night in and by about 22:00 (10pm) the shore patrol started bringing paddy wagons full of P-boat sailors back from the EM club.

Somebody evidently threw a beer bottle at one of our guys and then it was off to the races to find out how many of the other guys you could beat up.

I went down to the EM club the next night before heading to Hotel Street and it was totally destroyed. I was probably much safer on Hotel Street than on base.

This was one fight that I did not start and one that I did not participate.

Our next stop was Guam. This was the first time in port before Super Typhoon Pamela.

I was off the first night in port. A couple of signalmen and a couple of radiomen and me decided to head to the EM club at the Naval Station.

We commenced to get drunker than a skunk. Towards the end of the evening, we went out to get on the bus that was going to take us back to the ship. It was empty so we all took the back seats. The bus began to fill with Marines from our ship.

A couple of young Marines came on board and one of them was yelling at the top of his voice that he was going to knock the other Marine's head off. That is all that he did for about ten minutes. I finally stood up and yelled, "Take some action. Either knock his block off, or sit down and shut up."

That is all that it took. The one Marine hauled off and hit the other and that started a big fight among the Marines. The shore patrol came on board the bus and began spraying Mace. Some of the Mace hit me in the face and I could not see, but I also was not going to stick around and get my head bashed in with a baton.

I reached for the handle to the back door of the bus and opened it. I fell out of the back of the bus onto my side and the other four sailors followed suit and all fell on top of me. It probably looked like a Keystone cops movie. I finally got to my feet and grabbed the first cab to take us back to the ship.

From what I heard, many of the Marines were handcuffed and taken back to the brig on the ship.

This was a fight that I started but did not participate in. I don't think the Marines really knew who started it.

After our six week stay in Guam after Super Typhoon Pamela, we were off to White Beach, Okinawa. That place was probably not a bad place to be stationed, but it wasn't very good for liberty.

We had dropped the Marines off at White Beach for an exercise earlier in the day.

When we pulled into port, we knew that we had to depart early the next morning.

The Cleveland's (LPD) CO decided his ship was not going to enjoy liberty that night.

The Thomaston's (LSD) CO decided to allow his crew to go ashore on base only in civilian clothes.

Our ship's CO decided to allow us to go ashore on base only but we had to wear those stupid looking salt and pepper uniforms. That was back in the days where you really could not tell the difference between officers and enlisted unless you looked at the rank insignia on the sleeve of the enlisted.

With that in mind, there is already a conflict beginning to broil before the ship's allowed liberty ashore. One ship in civvies and one ship in uniform.

The base had an Enlisted Men's club where RM2 Johann (first name) and I decided to go. When we got there, many of the sailors were already three sheets to the wind. I decided to have a few drinks. I did not have a lot of money to get that drunk since I had just sent money home to Barbara for her to get our new apartment set up.

Over the next three hours, intimidation from the Thomaston sailors began to take a toll on the ego of a few of our sailors. The club was to close down at 2200. At about 2130 a fight broke out when one of the PO1s from our ship could not find his hat. He confronted a couple of Thomaston sailors. Next thing you know fists are flying along with chairs and tables. I decided to leave with Johann to head back to the ship.

As we were heading back we noticed several small fights ongoing. We just continued on until we came across a fight where one of the Operations Specialists from the P-boat was involved. Nunn was beating this poor guy in the face while the guy was biting into Nunn's finger.

This guy looked like he was in a lot of pain and so did Nunn. I yelled at Nunn not to hit the guy in the face but to hit him in the solar plexus. Once he did that, they guy would release his hold on the finger and Nunn could pull back. Nunn did that and then he kicked the guy a couple of times before heading off to the ship.

Johann and I continued back to the ship. As we were walking along a group of black sailors were nearby talking and joking. I noticed a couple of them were a Signalman and a Radioman from our ship and I nodded an acknowledgement to them. About that time Johann began calling them names. He used the "n" word several times and I told him to knock it off. As he continued, I told him if he did not knock it off, he was on his own. I grabbed him by the arm and he swung his arm around violently which caused me to release his arm and he bumped my glasses that went flying. I picked up my glasses, came back and hit him square in the face knocking his glasses off.

I left on my own to head back to the ship. As I neared the pier, I noticed two PO1s (one white, one black) beating on someone at the end of the pier. Before I got to them, they picked this guy up and threw him into the dirty harbor. A man-overboard alert was sounded. They finally fished this guy out of the water. I got onboard and knew right away that reports would be forthcoming to be sent out via radio.

I went down and changed into my dungarees and went up to radio.

I was up in radio for a while when in walks Johann. He was pretty beat up and his glasses were broken. He was still using the "n" word and telling me about how they had beaten him up. I just looked at him and told him that as long as he used that word that he would probably continue to feel the brunt of dark fists and shoes to his body.

That port visit ended in both COs being chewed out by the squadron commander. Fifteen Peoria sailors and 29 Thomaston sailors went to Captain's Mast for punishment. Reports from both COs had to go the squadron commander. I read all of them since they had to come through radio first.

The Fighting P-boat continued its fights throughout the rest of the cruise.

British Grenadier Soldiers Are Wussies
By Don Johnson, LT, USN (Ret), ex-RM1

This incident happened in Hong Kong about two thirds of the way through the 1976 deployment on the fighting P-boat.

I had been hanging with little Will Taylor who was much older than me and one helluva drinker.

We were nearly out of money having just left Subic Bay. Will went and borrowed a couple of hundred dollars from a Signalman. This guy had a slush fund and Will promised to pay him back at 100 percent interest. I did not know that for quite some time.

When we pulled into Hong Kong, Will and I had the first inport watch and planned to go on liberty when we got off at about 1800.

Wan Chai District

We took a water taxi to Fenwick pier and grabbed a taxi to take us down to Wan Chai District of town that had all the bars. We found a few bars and commenced to drink ourselves silly. In the last bar that we visited that night or next morning as the case was, we drank with a bunch of British soldiers. We drank and drank and drank. I must have drunk 12 pints of beer that night. I finally had to say that's it. I grabbed Will and headed out the door and hopefully back to the ship. I thought I knew the way back so we headed that way.

About two blocks down from that bar, we heard some guys yelling at us. I couldn't make out what they were saying and I just told Will to behave himself. It was 0430 and I was so drunk and close to being ill.

These guys came across the street for us and I had Will follow me down and across the street and began a trek down a side street when I saw what I thought was a short cut back to the ship. Guess what? The street was a dead end alley.

These guys followed us into the dead end alley and began to make threatening moves. I told Will to stay near me and I would try to talk our way out of this situation.

There were six of them, British Grenadier soldiers, I would find out later. They were supposed to be the equal to our Green Berets.

Will got scared and ran across the other side of the alley and two of the guys ran after him. They began hitting him with there fists and Will dropped to the pavement. I told myself that was enough. I ran across the alley to where they were. As I got there, one of the soldiers brought his foot down on the side of Will's head and I saw blood gush from his nose.

I grabbed that guy and knocked him to the ground and began stomping him in the gut with my foot and the last stomp I got in was in his groin. I knew that hurt him by the loud groan that he let out.

I then turned my attention to the other guy and began fighting him. All of a sudden there were several fists and shoes whipping up on me. I was shoved to the ground and looked up and there were five soldiers swinging fists and kicking with their combat boots. I just curled up in the fetal position and they had there way with me. They kicked me in the head, the back, the ribs and the legs. I had grabbed my crotch with both hands so they would not damage my love life.

When they were through, they picked up their buddy and left.

I laid there for quite some time trying to wake Will up. Then I passed out. I remember waking at one time and seeing some Chinese people standing around us. I told them in English that we were hurt and to call an ambulance.

Not long after that, an ambulance showed up. By this time I was fully awake and feeling no pain. They took us to Queens Memorial Hospital where they began working on Will. He was really groaning and making noises.

At about 0600, British MPs showed up. They were questioning me about what had happened. I told them what had happened. The MPs wanted to know if I could identify the culprits and I told them that it would be very unlikely right now since this happened so fast and since I was on the ground getting kicked to death.

About 0615, I looked down towards the emergency room where they had Will and I noticed some guys carrying a guy to the emergency room. I told the MPs that those were the guys that whipped up on us.

These soldiers had decided to bring their buddy into the civilian hospital to hopefully not be caught. Their buddy was the one that I had stomped badly. The other guy that I had fought with temporarily before I was thrown to the ground had a black eye. So I guess I got my licks in before they all decided it was time to put this drunken sailor away.

The MPs took the five soldiers away with them while their buddy was attended to in the emergency room.

Another MP came into the hospital in civilian clothes to take me down to their headquarters for further questioning. She determined that I had used self-defense in beating the one guy up and blackening the eye of the other one.

She told me that these guys were out looking for someone to beat up, because the night before Marines from one of the other ships inport had beat up several of their buddies in a fight. She also said that they would be punished. She then offered me a ride back to Fenwick pier.

I took a water taxi out to the ship. The galley was still open for breakfast so I went in and grabbed some. As I began to eat, I felt a lot of pain in my jaw. I mean a lot of pain. I know I looked like I had been run through a meat grinder, but this pain was terrible. I could not bite down on anything without a lot of pain.

I decided to go to sick bay to see the Chief Doc. He looked at me and told me that my jaw joints were probably just sore from being kicked around a little. I told him that I thought my jaw was broken, because when I bit down, my bottom jaw was not sitting right. He begged to differ with me, but decided to send me over the USS Dixie. They had a dental department on board with a panorex x-ray machine that could x-ray my jaw to see if was broken.

I grabbed a water taxi, went back to Fenwick pier and then another one out to the Dixie. When I got on board, the messenger of the watch escorted me to the dental department.

The dental techs told me that the panorex x-ray machine was broken and that they were unable to x-ray my jaw. Then they decided to send me over to the medical department and the x-ray technician was ashore. So guess what? No x-rays today from that ship.

I finally got back to the P-boat. My division officer had the medical doctor with the Marines look at me. That doc thought I had a broken jaw. So I went back down to sick bay and told the Chief Doc what the medical doctor said. He told me that I would have to wait until we got to Okinawa before he could do anything. I told him that I wanted treatment today or at least have my jaw x-rayed to see if it was broken. I told him that if it was not, then I would leave him alone. The Chief Doc told me to get out of his face.

I went back up to Radio. I noticed no one had delivered the CO's message traffic. I thought maybe I could get some attention that way. I know that he did not want any more attention from higher ups because at the time he had something like four Congressional Inquiries going.

When I got up to the CO's cabin, I knocked and when he said enter, I walked in and he saw how bad my face looked and asked me what had happened. When I told him, he asked if I had been down to sick bay. When I told him where I had gone and what had been done and what the Marine's doc had said, he called down to the quarterdeck and had the Chief Doc paged.

When the Chief Doc walked into the CO's cabin and saw me sitting there, he gave me a look that would have killed me if looks could kill.

The CO asked him why I had not received medical attention yet. When the Chief Doc explained to the CO what he thought was wrong, the CO reminded him that he was not a medical doctor and that I should receive immediate medical treatment. The CO called down to the quarterdeck and had the deck department ready his gig, so the Chief Doc could take me over to the British military hospital in Kowloon.

After I got in the boat, the Chief Doc began chewing on me about his plans with his wife being totally messed up now. I told him that if he had taken me to Kowloon earlier in the day that his day would still be good.

The first set of x-rays showed that there was a clean break between the left lower wisdom tooth and the molar. When the Chief Doc saw it, he looked at me and I told him that he was a lucky man and so was the CO, because if I had not received medical care that day, I was going to write my Congressman and tell him what happened. That break could have become gangrenous before we got to Okinawa.

The British oral surgeon asked me if I wanted a temporary fix or a permanent fix. A permanent fix would have left me in Hong Kong for at least six weeks if not longer. A temporary fix could be done that day and then I would be returned to the ship for further transfer to the Navy hospital in Okinawa.

I decided on a temporary fix. I had enough of Hong Kong for this cruise. I got drunk and got myself into a good fight. I opened a can of whupass on a couple of Britain's best soldiers before the others got me.

It took five of them to bring me down. What a bunch of wussies! Five on one!

However, I still have my love life and a jaw that is stronger now than before the fight. I also told myself that was going to be the last time I was going to do any serious fighting.

I have only been in two big fights since then. One was a couple of years after that when a seaman wanted to fight me for who was boss of the Radio Shack (I was a frocked RM1).

The next time was twenty years later when I beat up a would-be armed robber at an ATM in Sacramento who stuck a gun in my face to take my money. I knew he was going to shoot me so I took action before that happened. That third time felon is now behind bars for life.

Subic Bay, We Love You
By Don Johnson, LT, USN (Ret), ex-RM1

Subic Bay aka Sin City. Any sinful thing that you wanted, you could find in Subic Bay.

My sinful thing was San Miguel Beer. I was in love with the stuff. I thought it was the best beer in the world or at least the Philippines brand. It seemed to be a bit more regulated when it came to alcohol content. The Manila brand seemed to be unregulated. One day you could drink two of the Manila brand beers and be drunk all night and the next night drink 24 and not be drunk and be bloated all at the same time and sometimes the next day you would be suffering from Montezuma's Revenge.

I always tried to make sure I got the Philippines brand.

This particular time in port Subic and I believe it was in the year 1978 on board Peoria. We had pulled into one of the supply piers and put our bow ramp out to the head of the pier. The Captain wanted to put the quarterdeck at the bow of the ship on the bow ramp.

It was the second night in port that I went out with a couple of Operations Specialists and a Signalman. I can only remember the name of one of the OSs and his name was Tom Tower.

We all went to the Sampaguita Enlisted Men's Club for some San Miguel, dinner and a little musical entertainment. We sat there and drank hard liquor for a while. I think I was drinking Scotch that night.

About 2300 we decided to go over to the China Seas Petty Officers Club. Once we got there, we began ordering San Miguel beer. That is all we drank the rest of the night. I do not know how many we drank, but I know that we closed the club up and that we had ordered two beers a piece at last call.

When we left, I remember walking about a block and that is it. When I woke up the next day, I was told what I did from the time we left the China Seas until I put in my bunk.

As we were walking back to the ship, there were a couple of other sailors from another ship. I was told that I yelled expletives at them and my buddies thought that they were going to have to stand up to my honor. That did not happen. I guess these two guys were just a drunk as us and did not care.

When we got to the ship, my buddies went up the bow ramp. It was sitting at about a 45 degree angle. That is not too steep except when you are extremely drunk and don't know what you are doing.

I was told that I tried to traverse the bow ramp three times and each time I would get about half way up the ramp and I would fall and roll back down the ramp. After my third attempt, the Officer of the Deck sent the Messenger of the Watch down to help me up the ramp and then down to my bunk. I guess the Officer of the Deck and his watch crew and my buddies were having a whale of time laughing at me.

I guess we got back around 0300. Reveille went as usual at 0600. One of my radiomen said he attempted to wake me three times between 0600 and 0700. The last time he said I woke up, gave him the finger, yelled an expletive at him, rolled over and went back to sleep.

At 1300, my chief came down to the berthing compartment and began yelling at me to get up. I looked at my watch and asked him why someone did not wake me. He told me that someone did and that is when I found out what I had said and done to my radioman. The compartment cleaner who was a signalman told me that I did get up at 1000 and puked in the trash can and went back to bed. I don't remember doing that either.

I got up, took a shower and dressed to go up to radio. I decided to take the duty that day and next so I would not go out and get drunk again. I did not need to get myself into a lot of trouble since I was awaiting results of the PO1 exam.

I also found out that my chief had gone out the night before and helped close down the CPO club and that he did not get up until about 1100. He told me that when I make chief then I can do things like him, but until then I was to be up and ready to go at 0700 every morning setting a good example for the troops.

I do not think I ever got that drunk again in Subic Bay. I still have fond memories of that place because that was a place that you could let you hair down and get as drunk as you wanted without really getting into any trouble.

I love you, Subic Bay.

Our Beer
By Don Johnson, LT, USN (Ret), ex-RM1

I have wondered for many years why I did things that I did. My only answer is that alcohol took all of my inhibitions away.

When I was stationed at the Naval Communications Area Master Station Eastern Pacific (NAVCAMS EASTPAC) in Wahiawa, Hawaii, as an RM1, I did a lot of beer drinking. I drank a lot of scotch and I drank a lot of wine.

I worked at the Fleet Telecommunications Operations Center as a rotating watch supervisor for 7 months then I became the department Leading Petty Officer (LPO) and manager (I don't remember the title) of ensuring all large combatants received their Naval message traffic in the area they were going to operate.

But being the LPO of the department I had a lot of say in where we were going to hold our quarterly departmental picnic or luncheon or whatever we decided to do. Each department received so much Morale, Welfare and Recreation (MWR) funding for such get togethers.

Most of the time, we had beach parties and reserved a cabana at one of the local military beaches for those. We normally rotated between the beaches. The beaches were good for all of the various picnic sports that we had set up for the parties, such as volleyball, horseshoes, flag football, swimming, body surfing, etc.

I had a fairly good time being on the planning end of things, and almost always, the parties turned out to be successes. I liked that.

Sometime during the time right after I became LPO we got a sub-mariner RM1 onboard who knew very little about surface communications. He was made a watch supervisor and had to learn it very quickly.

Well, he wasn't fairing too well. His Communications Watch Officer, a warrant officer or Limited Duty officer (I don't remember who it was), came in complaining to the FTOC Division officer about him.

Well, the RM1 was selected for Chief Petty Officer. That got him off the hook, because RMCs did not stand rotating watches.

Guess what? We had no one to replace him, so guess who went back on the rotating watch bill? You got it. ME! I wasn't too happy about that.

I was also helping to plan the next beach party which was going to be at Dillingham beach, an old Army Air Force base beach and if I am not mistaken was one of the beaches that some of the Hollywood movies about Pearl Harbor were filmed. Dillingham Field was also used in the movie "Tora, Tora, Tora."

It was up at the far north part of Oahu and ended just before going around the northern tip of the island to the Waianae Coast.

RMC(SS) as I will call him now did not like me too well either. We were always arguing over something. Just because he was a Chief made him right all the time, or that's what he thought until he ran into me.

He was always trying to gross someone out at the departmental beach parties. Doing things that submarine sailors do.

On this particular Friday, the day of the beach party at Dillingham, I got up there early to start setting up and have things ready for when the main group began to arrive at about 1100.

I was setting things up and decided to pop a cold beer, one that I had brought from home. I sat it down on a picnic table while I was setting up.

I noticed that RMC(SS) showed up, around 1030, and was walking over to where I was. He stopped at the picnic table that had my beer sitting on it.

He wanted to know where the beer was and I told him that it was over being iced down since it was not cold when we bought it.

I know that he heard what I said. What does he do next? He reaches over and picks up my personal beer and takes a big swig.

I yelled at him that the beer was my beer. He said, "It ain't now; it's my beer." About that time he spit a big hocker right in the beer.

He was trying to gross me out. Being the type of person that I was back then, I went over to him, grabbed the beer out of his hand and spit a big hocker into the beer and took a big swig.

I said, "It ain't your beer anymore; it's our beer. Want to share?"

That did it. I had finally grossed the guy out. He took off to the rest-room. I did not see him for quite some time.

He finally showed back up and was quiet the rest of the day. He said nothing to anyone and neither did I.

I knew I had won the fight.

RMC(SS) never did bother me after that. He actually became a pretty good friend and would always ask my opinion of something before he would act, if he had a question on something professional about his job.

I am a sharing kind of guy and I don't mind sharing my beer if you don't.

You're Sick
By Don Johnson, LT, USN (Ret), ex-RM1

I have never been a really good drunk. I seemed to get sick more than pass out. It was probably because my body was telling me that drinking in excess was not good for me.

Being the sailor that I was, I did not listen to my body very often. It was one of those macho things. I couldn't let my buddies know that I was not a good drunk.

There were many times in my Navy career where my over indulgence made me sick. I did something different each time I got sick. I didn't want people to know that I got sick so I would try to find a way to either get away or to feign some type of illness.

I can remember the first night ever in Subic Bay; the guys were really trying to get me drunk. I was out with Mike Hancock, Bill Caisse, Dan Daniels, Vic Ficarra, a signalman named Vern and a couple of other guys I cannot remember by name.

We began drinking in a couple of clubs that Dan Daniels liked to visit. I was really trying to put the San Miguel away. After about eight beers and eating all types of food, I was beginning to feel somewhat nause-ated.

I was glad all the guys decided to leave this bar before I vomited. This was during the time before Zumwalt came out said that we could wear civilian clothing ashore. I had my liberty whites on. It had been raining that day which is normal for Subic Bay.

As we vacated the bar my stomach became more nauseated. Dan said "Let's head across the street." To get across the street you had to run, spin and jump around jeepneys (colorful taxicabs). As I was running, jumping and spinning, a jeepney bumped into me hard enough to knock me to the ground. As I was getting back on my feet, I felt my stomach begin to heave. I heaved, alright, all over the hood of the jeepney. The driver was mad and yelled at me to pay him to clean his jeepney. I just continued to run, spin and jump until I finally caught up with the rest of the guys.

I think back on that situation, it kind of reminded me of the pilot in "The Flight of the Intruder" when they were running from the shore patrol and the pilot asked the jeepney driver if he had room for a six pack and a pizza and driver said, "Yes." Then the pilot vomited in the jeepney and then left.

I can imagine situations like that happening all the time in Subic Bay.

Another time my wife and I were at a ship's Christmas party in San Diego. I got there and was having a good time chatting with my buds and introducing my wife to all of them since many of them had not met her just yet. There was a band scheduled to play beginning at 9 p.m. I was hoping it was a decent band and not to loud.

Our food that night was served buffet style and it was turkey and ham with all of the holiday fixings. We had a no host bar which was inexpensive by enlisted men's standards.

We were sitting at the same table as the CO and his wife, my chief and his wife and several of my buddies. I think my Division Officer was at the same table, too. As the night went on, the booze kept flowing and I kept drinking. I must have had about a half dozen double scotch on the rocks and a dozen beers.

About three hours into the party, the band began to play loud and my head began to spin and I knew at that time I was going to get sick. I was boxed in and could not get out in time to go vomit so I began to look for alternatives. The only alternative I found was to vomit under the table.

I tried to disguise my sickness by appearing to look for my missing wallet. As I bent over under the table, I got as close to the floor as I could before I let it go. I wasn't quiet either. I made several loud vomiting sounds and banged my head on the table several times. I am glad the band was playing loud.

My wife, Barbara, knew what I had just done. She said, "You're sick!" I said, "You got that right."

My chief, who would later that night be pulled over for DUI, knew what I had just done. He looked at me in disgust and shook his head sideways. A couple of my buddies knew that I had vomited under the table and they got up and went to a different table.

By this time I was able to stand and walk away from the table. I asked Barbara to come with me so that we could go home. She was mad at me because all I did was come to the party, eat, drink and get sick. She wanted to stay to do some dancing. I decided not to fight with her and told her that was fine. You stay and dance. I am going out to the car and sleep off this drunk. At 2 a.m., she is waking me to drive home. She had a wonderful night dancing the night away with all my buds. I know that she had a couple of drinks, too, but not like me. By that time, I was pretty much sober and was able to drive home. I lived not too far down the street from where my chief lived. I do not know what time he went home and when he got pulled over for DUI.

There were about three or four more times after I had become an officer that I got sick while on a drinking binge. I will tell you about two of those times.

One time was in San Diego. My ship had just returned from a WestPac/Indian Ocean deployment. My favorite music was once again becoming country western. At that time my two favorite artists were Kenny Rogers and Dolly Parton who were touring together. They were going to be in San Diego at the Arena about two months after we got back. I wanted to go see them so Barbara and I decided to invite her best friend, Linda and her husband, Jim down to go with us. Kenny and Dolly would be there on a Friday evening. I had to work that Friday and would not be able to get off too early.

When I got home, Linda and Jim were already there and Jim had been drinking already. I had a fifth of scotch and decided I wanted a couple of drinks before we left. I had two doubles. I thought that we could get something to eat down at the Arena. We left their two older children with ours and left in Jim's Camaro for the Arena.

When we go there, we each got us a jumbo dog and chips, not a very good meal, and each got a 44 ounce beer. I thought I could really handle this.

We got in to our seats and I ate my jumbo dog and chips. I ate the rest of Barbara's chips. I really downed that 44 ounce beer and wanted more. We never could get the beer sales guys up our way even though I kept yelling, "Beer here!"

Kenny Rogers finished up his part of the evening and then invited Dolly out to the stage where they sang their No. 1 hit, "Islands in the Stream" and a couple of other songs before Dolly had the stage to herself.

By this time I was drunk from the 2 doubles and the 44 ounce beer. I wanted more and finally Barbara let me have the rest of hers. I drank it and laid my head back and promptly passed out. I think Barbara was glad, because it shut me up. When the concert was over, I had missed the better part of Dolly's performance.

Barbara woke me and told me it was time to go. I wasn't going to argue. I just wanted to go home and sleep off the drunk.

As we were walking out to the parking lot, my head began to spin a little and I knew I was going to get sick. We continued to Jim's car. As we got there, I told everyone to get in the car and I would be right there. After they got in, I vomited behind his car so not to get any on it. People were walking by trying to find their cars and they were all watching me get sick. I finally got in and Jim was pretty drunk himself and he said, "It smells like vomit in here." I said, "What do you think I was doing outside the car? Speaking to the asphalt god? Let's get out of here."

Barbara and her best friend, Linda put up with a lot of my drunken shenanigans over the years. Linda finally divorces Jim after his drinking got out of hand and he started to become physical with her.

Linda finally met a guy that treated her like a goddess. Steve was a great guy. He drank a little and smoked a lot.

Linda had invited us down to her Southern California home to meet Steve for the first time. Barbara and I were living where we are now. We decided to go down on a long holiday weekend. I had just started my tour at Mare Island as an Officer in Charge, so I was kind of like my own boss. I set my own hours. We decided to head down on a Friday morning about ten o'clock and we arrived at Linda's apartment at about 4 p.m. She still had her son, Jimmy, still living at home. We were going to spend the night at Barbara's mother's apartment when we were through visiting for the evening.

Linda had told Steve that I was a true sailor and could drink with the best of them. She didn't tell him that I got sick a lot.

When Steve got over there at about 6 p.m., he and I shook hands and talked a little about our military careers. Steve had been Air Force for 11 years before he decided he couldn't handle the stupidity of some of his leaders and got out.

We had a couple of shots of scotch on the rocks while he was barbequing steaks on the grill. After dinner we sat down in the living room and began drinking beer. After about four or five beers I began to get nauseated and went into the bathroom. That was it for the rest of the night. I began to vomit. Before too long I had the drive heaves and I could not get up off Jimmy's bedroom floor. I had a towel that I was vomiting in. I could hear Steve out in the living room saying things like, "I thought this guy was a drinker? If this is what sailors are like, then I can out drink all of them." Linda was really trying to stick up for me. She had known me by that time for over ten years.

When I got up the next morning, I blamed the sickness on a new medication that I had been given a few days before. I thought it was a good excuse. So did Linda and Barbara. Steve was kind of skeptical yet. Jimmy told me that he was going to spend the night a friends' homes any time we came down from then on. Steve kept rubbing it in. He kept telling me that he could out drink any sailor if they all drank like me. I just let him have his field day with me.

Steve and I became good friends to the point that you could call us best friends. When I was doing my last tour of duty on the Indy, I would go up and visit with Steve and Linda on the weekend days that I could not go home. They eventually moved to San Diego when he picked up a General Manager position at a steel fabrication company there. My best friend, Steve, passed away a few years ago. I still miss him.

When I retired from the Navy in January 1992, I quit getting drunk. The most I drink now is a glass of wine with dinner about once every three to four months. I do occasionally have a glass of scotch on the rocks and that is it.

I have been sober now for over ten years. It is a great feeling getting up in the morning knowing you are not going to be hung over or having that feeling of nausea.

I am also glad that the Navy began to de-glamorize the drunken sailor back in the 1980s. As you can see from the various stories that it wasn't a pretty sight/site.

My re-newed Christian faith does not allow for drunkenness.

Chapter 9

Immoral and/or Unethical Acts

There was many a time that I saw immoral and/or unethical acts committed by enlisted and officers. I myself committed a few. I was not an angel. But as I started up the ranks upon re-entering the Naval service in 1976, I wanted to set a good example for my men and be able to lead them in every day Navy evolutions. It was not until about half way through the 39 months onboard USS Peoria that I began to mature as a senior enlisted man. It was then I began to square away my immoral and unethical character. It took becoming a commissioned officer before I really began to mature. I still drank alcohol, but not as much as I had as an enlisted man and I began to look at the UCMJ as a code that I really needed to abide by. I am afraid to say that many senior enlisted and officers especially senior officers felt they were exempt from prosecution under the UCMJ. I have some stories to tell you. I have left names out so that I do not embarrass anyone, but they will know who I am talking about if they read this book. These are stories I want to tell so that you as a reader know that some officers and enlisted men are not always on the up and up.

The first story is a lengthy story of my first duty station as a commissioned officer. I learned much in the short 19 months I was stationed there. All of the stories in this chapter are mine and are from my point of view. I am hoping that by the time I write the next book that some of these people will respond to me and I can put their response in that book.

My Worst Duty Station, Adak
By Don Johnson, LT, USN (Ret), ex-RM1

Adak Island in the Alaskan Aleutian Island chain is one of the most beautiful tundra laden islands anywhere. Its beauty was beyond reproach. The command that I was to report to was one of the worst that I had ever been assigned to and associated with.

Adak was going to be my first duty station as a commissioned officer. I went from RM1 to Ensign over night. The Navy did not want to send me to "knife and fork school" to learn the proper Navy officer protocol, but they felt I did not need it since I was former enlisted and that Adak would probably be a good place to learn it.

Were my detailers ever right when it came to learning Navy officer protocol on Adak?

My thoughts before I left Hawaii for Adak were that I would arrive and meet some great people and hopefully be able to learn the ropes as an officer very quickly. I also wanted to do everything by the book and to be faithful to the Uniform Code of Military Justice, Navy Regulations, etc.

I was commissioned an Ensign on June 1, 1982.

I took 45 days leave between duty stations. I had to find my wife and children a place to stay for about six to eight weeks while I was up there trying to set up a house for their arrival. They could not come up until we had a place to live. The waiting period was about six to eight weeks. They stayed with my sister which was probably the wrong place to put them up and not because it was my sister, but the timing of it. She was in the process of getting married again after a horrible failed first marriage. Everything did work out in the end and she still is my loving sister.

I was to report to Adak on July 15, 1982. On July 14th, I caught a flight from Sacramento to Seattle and from there to Anchorage. I had to spend the night in Anchorage before flying on out to Adak. I had worn my dress blue uniform from Sacramento to Anchorage and it was pretty soiled and wrinkly, so I decided to wear my civilian clothes on a civilian flight out to Adak.

When I boarded the aircraft, an old Lockheed Electra, a four-engine propeller driven plane, I was beginning to wonder where I was headed.

We left Anchorage at about 7 a.m. and arrived on Adak about midday or 1300. When I got into the terminal, I decided to wait for my baggage to be sniffed by a working dog before looking for someone to take me to the BOQ.

I was finally approached by someone who turned out to be my sponsor. This guy (I will call him JD) became a friend right away but later turned on me when things were not going so well for me.

The entire wardroom was there to greet me. The CO shook my hand and immediately told me that I should have arrived in uniform. I was to get my room at the BOQ, change into uniform and then report to him ASAP. The XO greeted me and I knew he would be no problem since he was leaving in about six weeks or so. It was not a good first day.

I wanted to check on my pickup before I went up to Naval Security Group Activity (NSGA) so that I could set up an appointment to pick it up right after my check in with the CO. I found that my truck was there, but the battery was dead. That was another bad omen for the day.

JD drove me to NSGA to meet with the CO. I was not looking forward to my check-in.

When I went to see the CO, he began to chew on me for not wearing my uniform from Anchorage to Adak. I tried to explain to him why I did not wear it, but he would not accept my reason. He told me to get my priorities straight and to report in the next day.

I stopped in to see the XO. He was not much of a talker. He acknowledged my existence and that was about it.

My third stop was to see my department head, Mike. He was an LDO, like me, but was a LCDR waiting to see if he made CDR and was going through a nasty divorce because of an affair he had with a junior female officer in his department. Mike turned out to be the best friend I was going to have for the next year to 15 months. He was going to try to protect me from the wrath of the CO and later the new XO as much as he could.

I was assigned to the Transmitter Site as the Division Officer which was located at the base of Mount Moffett. This was a remote location and many people liked it up there. They had turned the old vehicle garage into a club lounge type setting. Many NSGA events happened there during the summer months. The first CPO initiation that I was ever involved in as a defense counsel was there.

During the first couple of months I tried to fit in with the junior officer community of NSGA. I was having a difficult time. Some of the junior officers were much younger than me while the warrant officers and LDOs like me were a few years older than me. Seventy-five percent of the officers at NSGA were restricted line cryptology officers or warrants or LDOs from the cryptology field. The rest of us were unrestricted line or warrants or LDOs from the electronics or telecommunications field.

There was one cryptology LDO (I will call him CD) who was about my age but he was a bit too close to the CO. I found that out by accident one day.

One evening, I was in the club at NSGA with JD, CD and Arnie, a warrant officer, having a few beers. When I drink, I talk the truth. I do not cover my feelings. When I began asking questions about why the CO was the way he was, CD kind of stuck up for him. The CO's wife was a very heavy set woman and had a personality like a bent trash can lid. I would find out later why. But that particular evening as I was sitting having a couple of beers and trying to bond with my peers, I got kind of silly and wanted to know how the CO made love to such a big woman. No one said anything, so I told them how I thought he did and JD and Arnie laughed. CD just smirked. We drank one more beer after that and I was off to the BOQ down at the Naval Station.

The next morning I was called at my office at Mt. Moffett by the CO to report to his office. He did not tell me why I was to report. When I walked into his office 30 minutes later, I knew why. He began to yell at me for saying bad things about his wife and their sex life. He told me that I should never talk about a senior officer and his wife in a negative way. He never gave me a chance to say anything. He dismissed me from his office without comment.

I then went over to the Mike's office to talk to him about the situation and told him what had transpired. He wanted to know who was with me last night. As soon as I mentioned CD, he told me to watch my mouth around him because CD had become very close to the CO since his father had passed away a few months before.

I never talked about anything around CD ever again. CD knew that I knew he told the CO.

When I played on the Chiefs/Officers basketball team, we practiced down at the High School all the time. CD always wanted to be on the other team from me. He wanted to guard me all the time. He was a rough player. I was doing fine against him until one evening when I stole the ball from him and decided to drive the length of the court for a lay up. He stayed with me and as I went up, I slammed the ball off the backboard and in for a score. As I was coming down, he shoved me very hard and slammed me up against the concrete block wall behind the basket. That caused me a lot of hurt and when I went into the hospital the next morning still hurting, I found out that I had knocked some cartilage loose from my rib cage. I was out of action for the next month or so.

After about two months at this horrible duty station, my family showed up and we set up house once again.

We got a new XO and I thought that I might be able to gain some of my respect and honor back through him. At first I thought I had made some headway.

He was praising me for doing things by the book. I was rotated about once a month as a command duty officer (CDO). When situations came up that required to let the command's superiors know what was going on, I would call him and let him know that the book states this and that I should do this. He would then tell me to go ahead and do that. I would inform the CO and get his okay. Most of time if I told him the XO said it was okay, he would say okay.

One time I started watching the weather conditions and found that the wind was beginning to pick up. The CDO handbook stated that if winds hit a certain sustained speed over a period of so many hours that I was supposed to send out a naval message to certain commands letting them know that we were in a certain condition. I called the XO and then CO. I was applauded by the XO the next day for doing that. However, all of the other CDOs including the Master Chief chewed on me for doing that. They said that now they would expect them to be "by the book people", too.

I did not care. I was going to go by the book. However, this was going to be the last time I would do anything by the book, because I would be prevented from doing that by the XO and the CO.

I did an informal JAG investigation on a sailor who attempted suicide. They did not like my write-up. I recommended that the young sailor be given NJP because all he was trying to do was gain the command's attention that he wanted to go home. I had made a verbal comment to the command legal officer that if I was his parents, I would spank his bratty ass. NJP I thought was appropriate for this case. They let him off by getting him orders to the lower 48 close to his family.

I was assigned to the audit board. I was supposed to audit the books for the Morale, Welfare and Recreation (MWR) fund. All Navy Exchange profits were turned over to the MWR fund for departments and commands to do things for the sailors of the command.

One such thing they did prior to me reporting aboard was to buy a fishing boat for the command so that they could take groups out deep-sea fishing.

However, as I was looking at the books, I asked the MWR Manager about a couple of items in the book. One was money that was allocated to a cabin on the shores of Lake Andrew. I had thought this cabin was a personal cabin of the CO which would have made it illegal to use MWR funds to fix it up. The MWR Manager told me to not worry about that item. They were told to overlook that item. I was not about to. I then decided to ask the CO what was going on. When I did, I was told that the cabin could be used by anyone at any time for their use. I asked if he had a reservations listing so I could check to make sure that it was being used by others. He told me that he had none. I told him that this looked like an impropriety in the books. He finally told me to just overlook that item. That was exactly what I was told by the MWR Manager. I found out later from an enlisted friend of mine who worked at the NSGA Public Works Center that the CO had used Sea Bees to go in and fix the place up.

The CO had only used the place once for an officers' get together the entire time I was there. I even tried to reserve it a couple of times and was told that it was unavailable each time. When checking it out further, the CO was using the cabin for his use. That still stunk as an impropriety.

About two months after the new XO arrived, they changed all of the non-cryptology officers around to different divisions. I was assigned to the Tech Control Division where I should have been in the first place. JD had been the Division Officer. He was sent down to Naval Telecommunications Center (NTCC) Sweepers Cove at the Naval Station. Arnie stayed at the PatwingsPac Detachment for the P-3 Orion aircraft squadron (sub-hunters) that was home ported there. NSGA ran the tactical communications center for them. JD was not too happy about going to the NTCC.

I fell in love with Tech Control. I was allowing those people to do their job, something that had not been done in ages.

Once again doing things by the books would get me in trouble.

Adak had a bad early winter storm with winds hitting nearly 100 mph something they call a williwaw. This storm wreaked havoc on my transmitter site antenna farm. Five of my six directional antennas that supported the P-3 squadron had been damaged enough to put them out of commission. They were rotatable log period antennas. They were operated by remote control to rotate them to the sector required to support the P-3 aircraft.

The equipment casualty report (CASREP) system required messages be sent out when more than 20% of an equipment type was damaged and especially if it degraded the mission of the command. With more than 80% of my rotatable log periodic antennas (RLPA) gone, it was time for action. I was very familiar with the CASREP system since I was involved in a similar incident in Hawaii just two years before.

I drafted the CASREPs by the book, called the Officer in Charge of the Pat Wing Detachment to let him know that I was delivering the CASREPs to the CO for release so that we can get some immediate help.

I took them to Mike who said that we needed to do this in order to get the help needed. I then took them to the CO bypassing the XO since this was an operational matter and not an administrative matter.

The CO refused to sign off on them because he felt that by sending these reports out would place him on report for not doing his job properly. I told him that was not what this report was about. We had a storm.

The storm damaged the antenna farm, not sailors. He refused to sign off on them. He held them.

By this time, the OIC of the Det was getting antsy as to when those CASREPs were going out. I told him that they were not going out because the CO refused to put himself on report. The OIC was flabbergasted by that response. He called the CO direct and got the same answer. The next thing he did was take my information and sent out his own CASREPs addressing the issue with his boss and my CO's boss.

You want to talk about things flying. My CO got his butt chewed. The CASREPs sent out by the OIC of the Det were cancelled and regenerated by my CO who did not look favorably on me at all even though I told him what needed to be done. There was still a lot of heartburn about that situation for months to come. The transmitter site was turned over to the Electronics Maintenance Division Officer, so it was no longer mine.

That winter continued to plague me. On New Year's Eve, 1982, soon to be 1983, I had been over to a friend's house celebrating. Barbara and I went home right after the New Year came in. Not long after I got home, I received a call from the XO to go to the hospital since one of my men had been killed in a car accident on one of the back roads.

I got down to the hospital and found out that one of the young radiomen women who had been dating one of the electronics techs had been in the accident. She told me that he had lost control of the jeep and it rolled off the road throwing her clear. When she got up, she had noticed that the jeep had rolled over on top of him. She became hysterical and began walking over to the gate of the ammunition storage facility guarded by Marines. They helped her and got her to the hospital and finally got base security, the Sea Bees and medical personnel out to the accident location. They rolled the jeep upright, but the young electronics tech was dead. Both the young sailors had been drinking which added a negative to the already bad situation.

The XO came in after I ascertained all the information and began to chew on me for not controlling my people and look what happens when people are out of control. I looked at him and told him that both people work at the transmitter site which is no longer my responsibility and if it had been, this would not have happened. I told him to get off my back and get the division officer over here that was responsible for the transmitter site and the people. I turned and walked out. The XO never asked me what happened.

I was later transferred to NTCC Sweepers Cove to get me away from NSGA. I was causing too much trouble up there.

The CO of the Naval Station was a good guy and from what I could tell, he was a by the books type guy which made me feel pretty good.

NTCC was not a great place to be. I can see why JD complained all the time. The people who worked here all had problems. I played father, JAG investigator, counselor, and nursemaid most of the time I was there.

I had several incidents that really taught me some lessons. Only two of those will be written about in this book.

One was a time when I came into work one morning and I received a call from base security. They had an RM1 there that worked for me. He walked in and had reported that his wife, a Filipino, had hit him upside the head with a frying pan twice and then pulled a knife out and threatened to kill him with the knife. She then locked her two children into one of the bedrooms and threatened to kill them, too, if anyone tried to come into the house.

I went over to security and talked to them. They suggested I get a hold of one of the chaplains. I found out that two of them were off the island and the other was out on a day hiking trip and would not be back until later that day.

I then asked them what I should do. They told me that I could possibly utilize one of the drug and alcohol counselors to help out since they are trained to counsel people. The hospital did not have a psychiatrist or a psychologist assigned to it, so that was out of the question.

I finally decided to use one of the drug and alcohol counselors to try to get into the house to talk to the woman. In the mean time I had called my temporary department head, LT PE, (Mike had just transferred to Japan a month prior). Well, PE thought I was doing good job and to keep going in the direction I was going and that he would keep the CO and XO informed.

I got the drug and alcohol counselor involved. He called her up and talked to her for about ten minutes and finally got her okay for us to go visit with her.

When we got there, we knocked on the door and talked to her for a while. She finally let us in to talk some more. My main concern was to get the children out of the house for a while to defuse the situation a little. I did not want to see any harm come of them.

I found out that she did not like anyone with a beard. The counselor had a beard. She did not trust men with beards. I told her okay. I asked the counselor to leave and I would do what I could to defuse the situation even further and gain the release of the children.

I got her to agree to let the children go with me. I asked her if she wanted anyone to come over to keep her company so that I could put in place a counseling team that she could trust. She said that she would be okay by herself.

I took the children, a boy and a girl, with me. I took them up to the base chapel and went to get them some breakfast.

After I knew they were okay, I called PE to check in with him to let him know what I had done so far. He said that I was doing well.

I then went back up to base security and picked up the RM1. I told him his children were safe at the base chapel.

I began to get information from him about his life, his wife's life and about their marriage. He told me that he had met her in the Philippines, got married and brought her to the states with him.

He told me that their marriage had not been very good even from the start which had been about 18 years. She was hotheaded and sometimes went off on him for no reason just like that morning. I had asked him if he had ever considered marriage counseling and/or psychiatric counseling and checkups because she might have a mental illness that is causing her to act the way she is. He told me that she refused to go to counseling and refused to see a Navy psychologist or psychiatrist.

I then left him at the NTCC and went back to the base chapel. I talked to the children for a while and asked them a little about their mother. Both seemed to be somewhat afraid of her and both told me that she sometimes spanked them for no reason. That bothered me. I tried to find a place to put the children up for the rest of the day and possibly for the evening. No one wanted to get involved in this possible explosive situation. So I decided to put them up at my house with my wife and children. My family did not need to be a part of this, but I had no choice.

I then called up the children's mother and talked to her more and she told me that she was okay. I asked her if she wanted me to come back over and talk to her. She said that she was okay and to leave her alone for a while so that she can get herself together enough. I told her that her children were safe in my house for the time being and that I would have her husband put up at the barracks for a few days. She told me that was fine with her at that time. I asked her if she wanted me to have one of the base chaplains to come over and talk to her. She said no. I never even thought about someone from the Fil-Am Society going over to talk to her.

About 5 p.m. that evening, I received a phone call from the XO telling me to get my ass over to the RM1's house that there was a real problem here. I asked him what the problem was and he refused to tell me. I thought to myself that maybe she had committed suicide. I was now scared. He told me to pick up her husband and bring him over, too.

I went to pick up the RM1 and then over to his house. As we went inside, the XO, the president of the Fil-Am Society and his wife were sitting on the sofa. The Methodist chaplain was sitting in a chair at one end of the sofa and the RM1's wife was sitting in a chair at the other end of the sofa. He had us get two chairs and sit them opposite them.

After we sat down, the XO began berating me and the RM1 for making a total mess out of the situation today and told me that I got too involved in the case.

I asked him if he knew what had transpired today. He said that he heard what had gone on from PE, my temporary department head and from the president of the Fil-Am Society and from the chaplain, with neither having been involved in this all day. I was now getting mad.

I was told that I should not have gotten a drug and alcohol counselor involved in this since it was not a drug and alcohol case and that I should have involved a base chaplain in the case as soon as I could and that I had no right to take those children out of her house without her permission.

I was flabbergasted. I had asked him if he knew anything of what PE had told him had sunk into his thick skull. He told me that what he had heard from PE was all second hand information and not correct. I said, "Listening to these two people here who had no knowledge of what went on today is correct?"

I looked at her and asked her why she did not accept further help from me when I asked her. I had recommended the chaplain once he returned from his day hiking trip. I asked her if she wanted someone else to come over to talk with her. She just sat there and said nothing. Then she spoke and told me that she no longer trusted me once I took the children. I told her that I was afraid she would harm them. I told her that I wanted to no harm to come to them and that is why I asked her permission to take them. She said that I never asked her permission even though I did and she granted me that. I did not want to call her a liar in front of everyone and it took a big bite of the tongue not to do that.

Finally I asked the XO if he was finished. He said that he was not and I told him that I was. I got up to walk out and he told me that I would bring the children back over to her, now. I told him that I would ask the children if they wanted to come back. He followed me outside and ordered me to bring both of the children back over. He even asked me if I had learned anything today. I said I sure did. I learned that I screwed everything up all day long even while passing information to my department head that should have been passing it to the XO. I told the XO that at any time during the day if he thought I was not going in the right direction he should have told me so and I would have come to NSGA for further direction. I said I never received that, so why am I now being ripped apart for making my own decisions whether they were right or wrong. He told me to come to see him tomorrow morning and that we would talk then, but right now get the children back to their mother. I told him that if she harmed those children, I would find some way to have him prosecuted along with her.

I went and picked the children up and told them that they had to go home now. Both were apprehensive about going home.

That situation finally worked itself out. I was finally able to convince the woman that she needed to go in for marriage counseling. I do not think she ever got a mental checkout. Today I know much more about mental illness and I could probably diagnose her, but I will not do that here. I still wonder what ever happened to that RM1 and his family.

The next situation was a charge of sexual harassment against me.

I had another RM1 working for me as the training petty officer. One of the women in one of the rotating watch sections was not completing any of her training and not showing up for training on the days that she should have. When he began putting pressure on her, she went to her husband who was one of the base security patrolmen and told him about what was going on.

This RM1 and his wife had been at the Top Four club one evening and when driving home, he was stopped by this young sailor's husband for a possible DUI. He was taken down to the base security office where he became uncooperative because of the way he was being treated by this security patrolman. I was called by the RM1's wife who was in hysterics. I decided to go down there to see what went on.

I found out that the RM1 refused to do a breathalyzer. I said "Well then, why don't we take him to the base hospital for a blood test then if he feels that the breathalyzer is not accurate? The security patrolman told me that if the RM1 refused to take the breathalyzer then he would automatically lose his driving privileges for one year. I said, "Show me that regulation." He did and guess what? That is what it said.

During this time, the RM1's wife was giving the security patrolman a hard time. She was telling him that the reason you pulled him over was because of a disagreement that his wife and the RM1 had earlier that day. The security patrolman denied that. Then she went on to berate him for hitting on her earlier in the year when he stopped her for a minor moving violation. Again he denied that.

I finally got them to knock off the arguments. I got the RM1 to blow into the tube and he was still over the limit. The RM1 lost his driving privileges for a year.

Then I began to watch this security patrolman. He watched certain people and he sat in wait for them down by the Top Four Club and then stop them just before they got home.

I finally decided to counsel this young woman sailor myself, so I decided that when I did I would have my RMC and this young sailor's female supervisor sit in for my protection.

During the counseling session, I got a little heated and told her to quit acting like a bitch. I continued my counseling session and when it was over, I had her sign a statement that she would complete her training requirements within the month.

The next morning I get a call from the XO stating that he had on his desk a report accusing me of sexual harassment against this young female sailor.

He had asked me to come to his office to view the report. I did so and afterwards he asked me if I had called her a bitch. I told him that at times during the counseling session things got a little heated and I may have used the word, but I did not remember and at that time I did not remember if I did. I told him that I had two witnesses that sat in on the counseling session which the report did not mention. I told him to call the RMC and the RM2 in and ask them. If either one of them tells you that I used the word, then I will accept whatever punishment is coming my way. He smiled at me and called the RMC up and told him to come to his office and bring the RM2. He then dismissed me and told me to wait outside until after they arrived and then left.

I did that. When the RMC and RM2 arrived, they saw me sitting there and asked what it was all about. I just told them to go in find out. They were in there a little over ten minutes, came back out and left. The XO came out to get me and when we got back inside, he told me that I got lucky this time. Both the RMC and RM2 told him that I never used that word or any other cuss word during the session. He said that he would send the report back stating that the accusation was unfounded per two witnesses who sat in on the counseling session.

I did not say anything else. I went back to my office. RMC was sitting there with the RM2. I asked them if I did say the word and both said that I had. I then asked them why they had lied. They said they lied to protect me and to bring some discredit upon the young female sailor who had been so vicious to so many people at the NTCC and were hoping that she would be brought up on false charges. That never happened and I did get off because two people lied on my behalf.

I do not feel too good about that today because of my new found religious beliefs and at the time it went against everything I had been trying to do as a commissioned officer. Now I was kind of a hypocrite.

I was going to have to make up for it later in my career.

That young female sailor later came in to talk to me just before she left the island to have her baby in the lower 48 states. She was divorcing her husband. She wanted to thank me for being who I was and that she was sorry for all the things that she had put me and a lot of the people through. I then became truthful with her and told her what had happened. She told me that it would stay with her and never go anywhere else. To this day it has as far as I know.

The island of Adak will always be a part of my learning cycle. I felt the CO and the XO were a couple of very incompetent officers and even if they weren't, they should have worked with me more than they did. I felt like every major decision I made on that island, I was undermined and then put down. Somehow the XO turned on me after he had been there for a while. Was it because the CO disliked me? Was it because I questioned authority when I knew orders were not lawful? Was it envy because I could turn my divisions around and get my people to do things for me when other officers could not?

I took those lessons learned with me to use at later duty stations. They came in handy onboard Belleau Wood, at Mare Island and onboard Independence.

I thank the CO and XO of NSGA Adak for providing me with the leadership training that the Navy did not provide me in Pensacola like they should have.

The School of Hard Knocks is sometimes the best way to learn.

Reverse Discrimination During the 1970s
By Don Johnson, LT, USN (Ret), ex-RM1

I had been out of the Navy for about 2 ½ years when I decided to re-enlist and become employed again. I had just been laid off a job that I thought I was going to have for a long time, but that's what I got for thinking.

I was quickly assigned to USS Peoria, an LST, which I found out as soon as I reported aboard would be leaving on a Western Pacific deployment in nine days. What a way to return to the Navy.

The Navy was having its problems. It was having all types of difficulties in the race relations area of the Navy's social structure.

I had never had any problems with people of other races and to this day I still do not.

When I reported onboard, I found that I was immediately assigned to attend a couple of race relations workshops, one I remember was titled, "Cultural Expression Workshop."

About two days out of San Diego on our trip west to the Western Pacific, I attended the workshop given by a Hispanic Chief.

I got through the workshop without a hitch and did learn a little about what was going on. I guess the Navy a couple of years before had experienced race riots onboard aircraft carriers and a couple of oilers.

I had been stationed onboard an oiler, Guadalupe, in the early 1970's and we had black (now African-American) sailors, Oriental (now Asian) sailors, Mexican and Puerto Rican (now Hispanic) sailors and

Indian (now Native American) sailors. I do not ever remember any problems between any of us. This was now mid-70's.

I kept wondering what was going on with our Navy and the American social structure. Had the Vietnam War and all the liberals done that much damage to our military psyche?

My goal when re-enlisting was to stay for 20 years and to go as high and as fast as I could in the Navy system. Now how was I going to do that?

My tasks were to do whatever I had to do to get into some type of supervisory position to make that happen. I figured if I was some type of supervisor or manager then I would be promoted much quicker. I did not want to be the worker bee any longer. I wanted to be the leader.

When I reported onboard Peoria, I found the RMC working as the ship's Chief Master at Arms. The Master at Arms rating had not been created yet, so many sailors had to do double duty in their own rating as well as working as shipboard police officers.

The radio division had an RM2 who was the Leading Petty Officer and was also leaving in three weeks when we pulled into Okinawa. RMC told me that the radio shack was mine when this guy departed and that I had three weeks to learn the radio shack.

You want to talk about a challenge and stress to go along with it. Here it was.

That was my beginning to a new Navy career.

I pushed myself onboard Peoria. I wanted to be an RM1 when I left. I wanted to have a Communications Green "C" awarded to the ship. I wanted to have the best radio shack in the Pacific Fleet.

In the mean time I worked my tail and my men's tails off to get us there. The only thing was that they wanted some of the same things that I wanted. So it was easy to get them to follow.

I took three guys who had been on board for two years and were still seamen (E-3). None of them excelled to become a petty officer. I got them motivated and by the time they left the Navy two years later all three had become either a petty officer third or second class.

I was doing things that no LPO had done in the past few years. My radiomen were now competent watch standers and could answer any question or troubleshoot any communication problem thrown their way and all because I could and wanted to, they did, too. I was feeling great about everything that was going on.

In 1977, RMC and my Division Officer, Ensign Don Hurley, who just recently retired as a Commander in the Medical Corps, began submitting my name to the Sailor of the Quarter board. Three quarters in a row I was not selected.

I kept wondering why after seeing who had been selected. Each quarter there was a minority sailor selected. I kept wondering if they were selected for how well they did their Navy job or if they were selected for being a minority.

I finally asked my RMC what was going on with the selection board. He told me that I needed to go see the Senior Enlisted Advisor (now Command Master/Senior Chief).

Our Senior Enlisted Advisor was an Engineman Senior Chief.

We sat down and talked about their selection process. He told me that their process was fair and that they felt that each candidate was well qualified for the job.

I got upset with him at that time and asked him if he knew what type of job PO3 so and so did. He was a black PO3 who worked the laundry.

ENCS told me that he could only go by the write up of the person submitting the nominee.

I came unglued and told him about the PO3 and how he does not care about the enlisted laundry and that we were missing at least two full bags of laundry. We never found the missing laundry. It probably went over the fantail some night so he would not have to do it. The laundry we did get back was all wadded up and pushed back into the department laundry bags and sometimes still wet. When we got it back, it was so damp and wrinkled that we had to iron everything.

ENCS finally came clean with me and told me that he empathized with me on the subject but that his hands were tied. He told me that the CO had a directive from higher authority that the Navy select a minority sailor for Sailor of the Quarter each quarter if at all possible for the next year. That was during the year 1978.

I looked at the ENCS and said, "Now how do you think the white sailors who bust their ass on a daily basis would feel if they all found out about that? And if they did, I bet there would be more racial incidents than there are now. ENCS, I will get my just desserts some time in the future. You will see."

ENCS said that he knew that I would and to keep my head held high and that I would be rewarded when the smoke clears.

I never told anyone about our talk until a few years ago when I gave a speech on the Affirmative Action Programs of the federal government. I spoke about this and was mobbed by a few minorities afterwards telling me that they felt for me. They told me that was what was considered "reverse discrimination" and that I should have taken it to court.

I will never do anything of the sort. I know that I will get my just desserts, because I have God on my side.

I was eventually selected to be a commissioned officer through the Limited Duty Officer program. That was my just desserts for being passed over for selection as Sailor of the Quarter back then.

I made sure that all of my performance evaluations showed that I was nominated for command Sailor of the Quarter and that any time I was in a leadership role and filling a higher rate or billet position that it was reflected.

Blow your own horn when it is time to be evaluated. If your superiors don't know what you have really been doing, they will know after you tell them.

That incident did bother me for years and probably still does today especially when I see things on TV about racial quotas or Affirmative Action Programs.

I am not a racist. Many of the minorities who worked for me afterwards were promoted or selected for commissioning programs just as I was. I evaluated my people on the type of job they did and how well they did it. If you were lazy, guess what? But if you were willing to make a commitment and give a lot of time like I had done, you were rewarded with a great performance evaluation that would get you promoted.

Promote on merit and not race. We will have a better world for it.

I Am A Captain—I Can Do Anything I Want
By Don Johnson, LT, USN (Ret), ex-RM1

Have you ever wondered how power corrupts a person's outlook on life?

When I reported to Belleau Wood, the guy I was relieving warned me almost from the gitgo that he was having radio frequency interference from an illegal ham radio set on board.

I then asked him why we just could not shut it down. He said it belonged to the executive officer (XO). I said, "So?"

Once I relieved the other guy, Frank, I began to do some research to find out why the XO had this ham radio on board.

The XO was authorized to have his ham radio set on board while operating in the Third Fleet operational control area. We had a naval message from Commander-in-Chief, Pacific Fleet (CINCPACFLT) authorizing its use.

The only problem was that the unprofessional and poorly rigged antennas that he put up in the ship's high frequency antenna farms still interfered with shipboard external communications. He just refused to accept that his piece of crap of a system was interfering with the ship's ability to communicate with shore facilities and other higher echelon commanders.

The XO continued to use his ham set.

From what Frank told me, the XO never even gave it one thought to ask for permission to use the ham set in Seventh Fleet. Frank brought that up to him a couple of times and had gone down to discuss the interference issues a couple of times. The XO would listen with deaf ears.

I tried the same thing a few times. I showed him in black and white where he was in direct violation of a CINCPACFLT directive on the use of his ham set in Seventh Fleet. He told me that he was a Captain and could do whatever he so well pleased. This XO was a corrupt man. He did not care that he was in direct violation of the top Pacific commander's directive.

If he had received permission from CINCPACFLT, he still would have had to send out a Naval message to CINCPACFLT and the Naval Security Group Activity in Hawaii each and every time he used it. The message had to go out prior to him using it so that the Navy spooks (cryptology techs) could track him using high frequency direction finding (HFDF) equipment. They wanted to be sure he was not talking about classified information.

Now whether XO talked about when we were going to pull into our next port or not, I did not hear him divulge any classified information when I monitored his calls in which I did many times especially when he was interfering with our HF communications.

How do I know he was interfering? The XO was a pretty sharp ham operator. I know that he was searching for the best frequencies to use. He would search out those signals that he knew we were using and find one of his ham frequencies that was close enough to ours and begin to use it. Then his transmissions would bleed over into our transmissions. I know it was him at least twice. When I would call down to his stateroom and confront him about what frequency he was transmitting on, the interference stopped for a while. Is that coincidence or not?

Later when I was able to determine the frequency that he was transmitting on, I began to monitor his transmissions when I could.

I was at a loss as to how I could report this guy without jeopardizing my career anymore that it was already jeopardized from my last duty station in Alaska.

We pulled into Yokosuka, Japan towards the end of the deployment. I knew the CO (Mike) of Mobile Operational Training Unit (MOTU) 13. I had worked for him for a short period on Adak. I wished he had stayed during my entire time there, but that is not the Navy way.

I told Mike about what had transpired after he left Adak and now what was happening on Belleau Wood. Mike told me that it was his responsibility to work with ships that were having radio frequency interference (RFI) problems. He sent his Master Chief Electronics Tech over the next day to chat with our Electronics Maintenance Officer. While he was there, he noticed the "unauthorized" antenna on board.

Mike sent a "Personal For" message to our CO about the unauthorized antenna not even mentioning anything about RFI problems and that it should be removed immediately before he sent a message to CINC-PACFLT.

I was called to the XO's stateroom and he showed me the message. He wanted to know who this Mike was. I feigned surprise by stating that I knew who he was and that I did not know that he was now the CO at MOTU-13. I told the XO that I was going to have to call on him and have dinner with him before we left port. The XO still thought I had something to do with the message. I just shrugged my shoulders. He told me that I was "one of the most disloyal officers" that he "had ever had the displeasure of serving with" and "to get the hell out of my stateroom."

I did have dinner with Mike and his new bride that night and we talked and laughed about the situation. Mike did tell me that it was his responsibility to look for things like that on Navy ships.

The XO did get to use his ham set one more time before we left Yokosuka.

The night before we pulled out, the signalmen had to set up for some type of signal flag display for leaving port the next day.

The XO's antenna was attached to one of the signal lanyards, so one of the signalmen untied the bare copper wire antenna, rolled it up and laid it in a puddle of water. It stayed there through the night.

The next morning before pulling out, the XO got up and fired up his ham set at 1500 watts and began to talk. From what the signalmen told me, the antenna began to smoke for a bit and then began to arc and spark. The feed back into the power amplifier of the transmitter caused major problems causing the power amplifier to burn out internally.

The XO immediately went to the signal bridge and what he found made him very mad. He immediately called down to the bridge and had the Boatswains Mate of the Watch page me over the announcing system. As soon as I got to the signal bridge, he began pointing to his smoking antenna. He was so furious that he threatened me with Captain's Mast for destroying his personal property and that I owed him $1,500 for the power amplifier. Luckily the Senior Chief Signalman was present and came over and told the XO what had transpired. The signalman who took the antenna down and laid it in the puddle also came over and verified that he was the one who laid it there not knowing that it was his antenna. The XO went storming off the signal bridge.

The Senior Chief looked at me and smiled and then I smiled at him. We then did a high five and began to laugh. The Senior Chief knew about my battles with the XO over that antenna. The problem was now gone.

My radio shack had one of the nicest and fairly non-stressful rides to Hawaii knowing that they were not going to have to worry about RFI from the XO's ham set.

I have looked back on that situation many times since and always wondered what made him think that he could get away with disobeying a CINCPACFLT directive. "I'm a Captain; I can do whatever I want."

I have known many Captains over the years and 90% do not have that kind of attitude. The Belleau Wood XOs seem to have had a problem with power. Many had been former COs of smaller vessels and I guess the power they had there followed them to the Belleau Wood.

Cut Them Off, A Story about a Random Urinalysis or Two
By Don Johnson, LT, USN (Ret), ex-RM1

This story is about another Belleau Wood XO who was on a power trip.

When I first met him, I thought he was a great guy. He worked with me on my Surface Warfare Officer qualifications. He was an excellent ship driver.

It was after you got to know him that you began to see his power trip. I found out more about him after I left the ship to become the Officer In Charge of the Naval Telecommunications Center at Mare Island, CA. I had a Master Chief Radioman working for me that knew him from two previous commands and I will tell you about that later in the story.

On this particular morning at Officer's Call we received the word on a random urinalysis that had to be conducted that day. Random urinalyses were just that, random. In the CMAA office that morning a pair of dice were rolled to come up with a number and that number would be the last number of the social security number. I don't remember what number was rolled that morning, but I knew that a number of men from my 50 department would be going down to take care of business that day. It was also standard procedure that the urinalysis was to be conducted from 0800–1700 which meant to me that you could go down to pee in the bottle anytime during that time frame.

My Communications Department had their muster and quarters station within ear shot of Officer's Call on the flight deck just aft of the island superstructure.

The XO directed all officers to get their men down to "I" Division berthing as soon as possible after muster and quarters. Now what does "as soon as possible" mean to you. I know what it meant to me. Sometimes it is hard to get all of your guys down there right away. I tried my best to get most of the guys down to the urinalyses before noon even my guys who were TAD (temporary assigned duty) to other departments.

On this particular day I had two of my guys, an SM3 and an RM3, working as side cleaners for the Deck Department. They were down there before quarters already working. They were told by their Deck Department supervisor, a BM2, to go take the urinalysis at lunch time.

This is where the power came into play. The XO called down to "I" Division berthing at noon and told the CMAA to cut the urinalysis off and anyone coming in afterwards would be placed on report for disobeying a lawful order and sent to Captain's Mast, non-judicial punishment.

My two TAD guys got down to do the urinalysis at 1205, five minutes after the XO called to cut off the test. I thought that was playing dirty pool.

The XO's reason when I asked was that many dopers were able to flush drugs out of their systems by drinking huge quantities of water throughout the day and then go down to pee in the bottle at the end of the day or they would find something to mask the drugs such as drinking vinegar or using other things that dopers know will mask the drugs.

That told me that the XO was out on a witch hunt and was going to burn whoever he could regardless if they were dopers or not. That was not right with me.

The SM3 that was placed on report was on the XO's witch list anyway. The SM3 had been out on the town a few months before and had gotten into a fight with the XO's yeoman. The SM3 beat him up for some reason that escapes me. I know the XO wanted to get this kid really bad and now was his chance. I was not about to let the XO get him.

I set up a time to go see the XO before I did my Division Officer's investigation.

When I went in to see the XO, the XO already had his mind made up to send these two guys to the Captain. He grabbed the two service records out of my hand and told me that he was sending them to Captain's Mast.

I pulled the service records back out of his hands and said that if that was the way that he wanted it, then I was going to do everything the Navy way and that was to do my Division Officer's investigation first, then pass everything up the chain from there.

My department head was kind of a "yes" man, and liked the XO just as I had prior to this incident. So my report went to the XO. The XO did not even hold an XO's investigation. He just sent the reports to the CMAA for Captain's Mast.

A few days later at Captain's Mast which was held at in the foc'sle (forecastle) I had brought down several witnesses to testify about the wording of the XO's Officer's Call orders that morning. I had my RMCS, an RM1 and an RM3. I also had another Supply Division officer there to testify on my men's behalf. The BM2 in charge of my two men was there to tell the Captain what he was told and what he told my men.

The XO got to testify first and he stood up there and lied like a big dog saying that he had told everyone at Officer's call that morning that all hands that had to participate in the urinalysis had to be done by noon.

I finally had had enough. I raised my hand and was recognized by the Captain. I told him that I had to butt in because I was not going to let the XO stand there and tell a bare face lie.

I told the Captain that I had brought several witnesses down to testify about the wording that morning and that I was not going to see a couple of my best men be railroaded by someone who had a power problem.

The Captain told me to shut up and then gave out a suspended sentence of 5 days restriction. That really made me mad.

I went storming out of there.

Shortly after all Captain's Mast cases were completed, the XO called me down to his cabin. He commenced to chew on me and I was so mad he made me cry tears and it was not from feeling sorry about my situation. He thought that he had me, but he did not.

The CO then had the word passed for me to lay to his inport cabin. I did so as soon as the XO threw me out of his stateroom.

The CO had me sit down in front of his desk and then asked me why I was acting the way I was. I told him that the XO is responsible under the UCMJ to not perjure himself during cases such as this. I told him that I would not have had all of those witnesses there if I had not been afraid of the XO lying about this case. I also told him that I did not want to see black marks go on my men's records because some senior officer lied at a Captain's Mast to save face. The Captain then told me that he only dished out the punishment to save face for the XO and that he would in six months have the NJP expunged from the records of those two men if they kept their noses clean. I left the Captain's cabin feeling like I at least won a little something that day.

Two weeks later at Officer's Call the XO told us that we had a random urinalysis again and that all officers were to personally gather all of their men and take them down to "I" Division berthing for the urinalysis as soon as possible after muster and quarters. My Department Head heard the same thing I did and so did all of the people at muster that morning.

Right after quarters, the XO grabbed me and told me that he wanted my RMCS, RM1, RM3 and me to help the CMAA with the urinalysis. I told him that we had many operational things going on to get ready for the next underway period and asked that the RMCS and RM1 be excused. He said definitely not. Since we all were there at that Captain's Mast to testify against him, he wanted us to go down and observe so that we knew how a urinalysis was conducted. Being the good officer that I was I gave him a hearty, "Aye, Aye, sir."

Everyone was just flabbergasted. We all knew how a urinalysis was conducted.

I had RMCS gather all of our guys that were to pee in the bottle that morning and we all four took them down with us.

RMCS and RM1 were charged with checking IDs and handing out the bottles. RM3 was an observer. He had to watch everyone assigned to him pee in the bottle. I was assigned to help the CMAA who was not too pleased with us being there. As a matter of fact, he was not too pleased with the way the XO has handled the last few urinalyses. He said that he was just following the XO's orders because he wanted to make Senior Chief.

Everything was going along just great until about 1030 when the XO called down. I answered the phone and the XO asked how it was going and I said just fine. He asked to talk to the CMAA. I gave the phone to the CMAA who said, "Yes, sir." The CMAA looked at me and said the XO said to cut off the urinalysis. I told the CMAA that was not right. He agreed, but said that he was just following orders. I thought to myself that this guy is not a strong person. I said, "Okay, I will go tell my RMCS and RM1 to start gathering up ID cards and filling out report chits."

When I told RMCS and RM1, they did what I told them. I stood behind them and as people came through they were told they were on report for not reporting by 1030 on orders of the XO. By the time we got done, we had a report chit on a Marine Master Gunnery Sergeant (E-9), a LCDR, supply type, who brought down his entire division at about 1045. He was madder than the devil. We had some other senior people including officers.

After it was all over, I took the list of names to the XO and the Captain. I told the XO that I would be glad to testify at the Marine's and LCDRs Captain's Masts since I was down there when he called down to cut off the urinalysis. He told me that he had given that order to the CMAA at 0700 that morning. I told him he was liar and that I had already asked the CMAA what time the XO told him to cut off the test and was told that he had no time to cut it off until the XO called down at 1030. Once again I was thrown out of his stateroom.

I immediately went to see the Captain and told him what had happened. He said that he would take care of it.

I left the Belleau Wood a couple of months after that for Mare Island.

About a year or so after arriving at Mare Island I had an RMCM come TAD to me because of a medical condition. As we began to find out a little more about our careers, I found out that he had served under this XO onboard two other amphibious ships, names to be unnamed.

On the first ship, the RMCM was an RM1 and was going through message traffic one morning and saw a random urinalysis results message. One of the SSNs was the XO's. RMCM told me that he began inquiring around the amphib base and found out that this XO had a drug problem and that it stemmed from duty in Vietnam as a special boat unit officer.

From what RMCM was telling me, the Navy did send him away to a drug rehab facility where he was cleaned.

We both thought that what he was doing on Belleau Wood was making up for his early on deficiencies in the Navy by trying to make the Navy drug free under the zero tolerance policy.

I had no problem with that; however, there is right way to do things and a wrong way to do things. He was doing everything the wrong way and out doing a witch hunt. You don't do that. I could have used my influence with a friend at COMNAVSURFPAC if I had wanted, but I did not. I knew a Commander from a previous duty station that would have filtered information upstairs as to how this XO was doing these random tests, but I did not want to do it that way. I thought I could handle it by using my influence onboard the ship.

Everything worked out okay for my guys. I found out later that the Captain kept his word and expunged the NJP from their service records.

Chapter 10

A Tribute to Navy Wives

September 14, 1970 was a great day in the lives of many Navy wives. The Navy wife was finally recognized as someone important in the life of the married sailor. For many years if the sailor's wife had a problem at home during deployment, many senior enlisted and officers could care less. A term used by many still burns me today.

"Your wife was not issued with your seabag so it's not our problem."

Retention was going down and one of the reasons was that many married sailors were getting out so that they could spend more time with their wife and children. Many may have stayed in the Navy if they had shorter deployments and if the Navy offered more assistance to their families while on deployment.

Admiral Elmo Zumwalt did recognize the Navy wife on September 14, 1970 in one of his famous "Z-grams" by setting up a Wives Ombudsman program. I quote from the first paragraph of the "Z-24".

"1. THE IMPORTANCE OF THE NAVY WIFE AS A MEMBER OF THE NAVY TEAM CANNOT BE OVER EMPHASIZED. ALTHOUGH THE WELFARE OF WIVES HAS ALWAYS BEEN OF GREAT CONCERN TO THE NAVY IT HAS BEEN NOTED THAT THESE DEDICATED

WOMEN HAVE NEVER HAD AN OFFICIAL REPRESENTATIVE TO
EXPRESS THEIR VIEWS TO COMMANDING OFFICERS AND BASE
COMMANDERS."

As your head hits your pillow tonight and you are thinking of your husband, think about this prayer.

<u>A Navy Wife's Prayer</u>
<u>by Anonymous</u>

At night when I crawl into bed,
My lonely pillow 'neath my head,
I close my eyes and say a prayer,
God keep him safe over there.
And God please make the time fly by,
And make me strong so I won't cry,

It's kind of hard to be alone,
And teach the kids when they're half grown,
Without the strength of a fathers hand,
To guide them in this troubled land,

So I'll need a lot of help from you,
to let me know what I should do.
And please God won't let him know,
How much we love and miss him so!

And then I feel across the bed,
To where he use to lay his head,
And close my eyes so very tight,
So I won't cry again tonight,
And whisper to the evening air,
Goodnight my darling over there.

Roses of Steel
By Debbie Benware

The United States Navy Wives are indeed "ROSES OF STEEL!"

Ask any sailor on any base in any part of the world what keeps him going, and he will answer, "My Wife!" Do not ever take your title lightly, for you are the backbone of your sailor. Not every woman can do this. It takes a special woman to stand behind her man when he is out to sea for months at a time. It is the spirit and stamina in you that helps you face the physical and mental challenges of everyday life. Oh no, not just any woman will do. Only a STEEL ROSE can handle this challenge. The Navy Wife!!

Can just any woman stand on the pier with babes in arms, and one on the way, and keep a stiff upper lip as she waves good-bye to her husband, keeping back the tears for "the children's' sake"? Can just any woman lay alone night after night, for months and months at a time being sole guardian of her family? Can just any woman get 2 weeks notice and pack up her whole household, pass a white glove inspection, load the car, say a quick good-bye to girlfriends who became like sisters and take off for yet another duty station only to begin all over again? Can just any woman take the loneliness and heartbreak of having no tender kisses, gentle touches, or sounds or smells of her husband day after day? Can just any woman take a set of whites and iron and starch them just the right way so her husband can pass inspection? Can just any woman be mother, doctor, maid, chauffer, umpire, psychologist, financial consultant, tooth fairy, Santa, the Easter Bunny , the main disciplinarian, and STILL enforce the love and discipline of an absent father?? Not likely!! So ladies, give yourselves a pat on the back for your strength, your dedication, your deep love for your husband and your country, for without you, where would your husband be today? Whether he is a seaman recruit, petty officer, Chief, Ensign, Commander, or Captain, he is what he is and where he is because he had a great woman standing right beside him, _you_, a STEEL ROSE of the Navy.

LOVE THOSE HOMECOMINGS!!!

The Real Invisible Women
By Theresa Davis

We sit at home waiting for the news…
News of our next "home", of our friends we will lose…

We plan trips…
Only to hear, "sorry baby" roll from his lips…

We stand on docks and wave goodbyes…
With tears in our eyes…

We tell lies, nothing is a mess…
To save him the stress…

We listen to babies cry for their daddies…
We withhold all of our worries…

We have babies, do laundry, and move one more time…
All of this we do without little more than a dime…

We wait for homecomings…
Only to dread the leavings….

We iron uniforms, drop off dress blues…
We find the ID card he always seems to lose…

We love them, cherish them, and into the military we marry…
Knowing that we will always come second to the military…

We do this for our country, for the one we love…
Only to be looked down on, as if you are somehow above….

Invisible, yes, sometimes we choose to be that way…
When he leaves us, some things we choose not to say…

"Please don't leave again! I need you with me here!"
We always seem to hide every single tear….

But today, my words I will say…
Invisible I will not be today…

We are PROUD NAVY WIVES….
And that we will be for the rest of our lives…

The Silent Ranks
By Anonymous

Contributed by Don Johnson

I wear no uniforms, no blues or whites,
But I am in the Navy cause I am his wife.
I'm in the ranks that are rarely seen,
I have no rank upon my shoulders.
Salutes I do not give.
But the military world is the place where I live.
I'm not in the chain of command, Orders I do not get.
But my husband is the one who does, this I can not forget.
I'm not the one who fires the weapon, who puts my life on the line.
But my job is just as tough. I'm the one who's left behind.
My husband is a patriot, a brave and prideful man.
And the call to serve his country not all can understand.
Behind the lines I see the things needed to keep this country free.
My husband makes the sacrifice, but so do our kids and me.
I love the man I married. Soldiering is his life.
But I stand among the silent ranks known as the Navy Wife.

Sleep Deeply
By Theresa Davis

Sleep deeply
My baby
Hold me in your dreams
Only in dreams or thoughts it seems
Play with my hair
Sleep without a care.

Sleep deeply
My baby
Restful night
Holding you tight
What a delight
Keeping you within my sight.

Sleep deeply
My baby
Miles may keep us apart
But you will never leave my heart
Here my baby
You will sleep deeply.

A Sailor's Prayer
By Anonymous
Contributed by Don Johnson

Dear God,
Watch over her for me,
that she may safely guarded be.
Help her each lonely hour to bear,
as I would lord if I was there.

When she is sleeping watch her then,
that fear may not her dreams offend,
Be ever near her though the day,
let none, but goodness come her way.

Sweet faithful girl who waits for me,
beyond the wide as spacious sea.
Be merciful, O God, I pray,
take care of her while I'm away.

The Wife
By Theresa Davis

A wife, a listener that is what she is...
One left at home, to move, to shop...
To take care of the kids...
To mow the lawn, take the car to the shop...
Someone to keep the lights on...
To keep the home fires burning....
Never to lose hope in him, make sure all is done...
To never lose sight of his loving...
She sits at home and waits...
For the call she longs for each night...
Thinking about all of his different fates...
Missing everything, even the fights...
Hoping it won't be long,
till she can hear the words coming from his lips...
She will be in his arms...
As the words "I love you" rolls over his tongue as he kisses her lips...
And again, as the lights turn off and she falls asleep in his arms...

Distance but Nearness
By Theresa Davis

Your voice, God so lovely it sounds,
fills my lonely ear with such sweet sound.
Over the phone, the only medium we share now,
it flows like soft music.
Our love, the thing I cherish and hold closest,
keeps me strong as my loneliness mounds.
The love we share now and for eternity burns so bright
as thousands of flames on top of candle wicks.
Alone every night, I lie in our bed, close my eyes tight,
and pretend you're holding me near.
Dreams come then, ones of our future together,
the wonderful times we'll share.
Down my cheek flows a river, one after another, tear after tear.
The love we have is one of a kind;
the love we share will be only ours, very rare.

My days
By Theresa Davis

My day began by opening my eyes and seeing your sweet face, eyes
closed, lost in a dream somewhere.
You sense my gaze upon you and opened your wonderful bright eyes.
I stroke your face, as I kiss your lips and run my fingers
through your hair.
Then suddenly you disappear, as my dream dies.

You're not here this morning, your country called you
and you ventured away.

I walk to the closet, run my hands over the little bit of clothes of yours
that remains.
Grabbing a sweater, I try to breathe in a bit of you, but the sweater has
long lost scent of you since last fall.
Just as your pillow that remains on our bed isn't yours anymore, your
head hasn't been on it in some time now, and this sends me pains.
Out of the room, I hope to leave my misery
but still it waits for me in the hall.

You're not here this morning, your country called you
and you ventured away.

To the bathroom for my morning shower, I grab a towel and knock
over your shaving kit.
I pick it up, a vision of you standing in front of the mirror, white
cream on your face, giggling and wanting a kiss.
Shoving past you, I would try to avoid that face, getting out of the
room with a playful hit.
Add this to my long list of things I miss.

You're not here this morning, your country called you
and you ventured away.

Hurrying to get dress and out the door, I'm late again, caught in all of
my memories of another time and place.
Grabbing my purse, turning off the lights, and to the door I run.
I take one more glimpse around, making sure everything is as it should
be, I catch a shadow of your face.
Opening the door, it fades away with the appearance of the sun.

You're not here this morning, your country called you
and you ventured away.

Nature, help
By Theresa Davis

Nature, I call upon you for help.
Memories of him I have kept.
You see, my baby left to protect our country.
Help me convince him I love him, please help him see.

Take the brightest star,
Send it to him no matter how far.
On the job, your strongest wind,
Catch his sail, to me please send.

Lightening bugs with the strongest flight,
Send them too please, to be his light.
Doves of love send to guide.
On their backs, he may ride.

Dolphins so friendly send them too,
They will know what to do.
Since I'm asking, how about a parrot?
"I love you" the words he will recite on his shoulder he will sit.

Send it all please.
Help me please.
If he can't come home to me,
To him bring a piece of me.

A Navy Wife's Prayer
By Sue Combs

How often we've stood on dark flight lines and piers...
"I love you", "I'll miss you" whispered through tears.
During long separations, in peace time, at war...
my nights filled with dreams of this man I adore.
With only my memories to hold close at night...
I live for the day God returns my sunlight.
Yes, life goes on when your loved one's at sea...
but the ache never leaves, the fear stays with me.
Dear Lord, I need Your guidance, Your love...
help me be brave, keep Your watch from above.
Hold my dear one so safe in Your heart and Your hand...
bring him home to his family...this hero...my man.
In us Lord, I pray he'll be filled with such pride...
of how we carried on without him by our side.
Please, help time fly quickly and soon I will hold...
the hand of the man whose eyes chase the cold.
Whose voice brings delight, whose touch eases pain.
How will I ever say "Farewell" again?
With Your help dear God, I'll try to stay strong...
and pray that his time here at home will be long.
Still, "I know that the Navy will need him", I sigh...
but we'll face it together, Dear Lord, you and I.

Any man who may be asked in this century what he did to make his life worthwhile, I think can respond with a good deal of pride and satisfaction, "I served in the United States Navy."

John F. Kennedy

Contributors

Debbie Benware: I am a retired Navy Wife of over 22 years. My husband and I physically retired from active duty in the Navy in Dec. 1988, but as "civilians" we are still quite active. My husband's name is John. He was a Senior Chief Machinist Mate and was piped over the side while serving on board USS Detroit, which was home ported in Norfolk, VA. You can read more about his Navy Career at http://jbenware.freeservers.com/. He is and always will be "My Senior Chief!" We raised four boys while in the Navy. Kevin, Brian, and twins, John and James. We traveled from Maine to Florida, to Great Lakes, to Virginia and made a few round trips in between.

Vern Bluhm: I am retired Air Force and Civil Service from Mare Island Naval Shipyard. I started out as a Navy radioman, then was shifted over to being a radarman (RADAR was fairly new at that time) and was a tail gunner on a torpedo dive bomber (TBD) off the original Saratoga in WWII. I spent most of my time on board USS Saratoga CV-3 with a 3-month stint with the Marines at Guadalcanal. I am now retired and spend all of my time doing volunteer work for my church, Toastmasters International and the Boy Scouts of America. I can be reached at vernbluhm@aol.com.

Sue Combs: I was born and raised in Dayton, Ohio. A graduate of Wright State University, I married my husband and best friend Bill in 1978 and soon became a proud Navy wife! Bill joined the Navy that same year and will retire in 2005. He is a Naval Flight Officer, having served on 3 different aircraft carriers and in several joint military positions. His duties have allowed us to travel extensively across the USA and to have had a small taste of Europe as well. Due to our many moves, I have enjoyed a rather "eclectic" job resume, both paid and as a volunteer. Bill and I are the proud parents of Daniel, a college student who knows everything there is about computers, and have only recently applied to adopt a little girl from China! We are presently stationed at Wright Patterson AFB, Dayton, Ohio. Yes, after 24 years of military "spouse hood", I have come full circle…back home where I started!

Theresa Davis: I have been married to a sailor since 1998 but he joined the navy in 1999. I'm 26, no children. I have an associates degree in Accounting and Business Management. We are in Mississippi at this writing. I was raised in Louisiana by my father.

Dave Foley: I joined the Navy in 1979, wound up on the Indy from March of 80 until September of 83. I did a second hitch as Brig Staff in Newport, RI. I got out after PNA'ing (Passed but Not Advanced) for PO1 twice and getting denied cross rating to MAA twice as well. That was in July of 1987. Wound up getting a job in my home town after many unsuccessful attempts with the Feds. I've been working as a Deputy Sheriff / Correction Officer for the past 15 plus years. I'm still married to my High School Prom Date, 21 years in August.

Steve Hawkins: "Plank Owner" U.S.S. Haddock SSN621, Ex-RM2(SS). I am married with two grown children and two beautiful grandchildren. For fun I am a Ham Radio Operator, WV6U, and radio collector (this borders the fine line between hobby and obsession), and I home brew beer. I have spent the last 30 years as a TechnoNerd in the Computer/Telecommunications Industry.

William Hughes: I served on active duty in the Navy until 1962, when I retired as a Master Chief Radioman. I served a short stint in Dallas regional office of the FBI during which time the assassination of President Kennedy occurred. I received a commendation for my service during the investigation following the shooting. I left the FBI in 1963 and became a Telecommunications Supervisor with a Major Oil Company from which I retired with 19 years service. I became an avid Amateur Radio Operator in 1949 and still have a valid license bearing my original call sign—W5PYU. As a radio "ham" I provided emergency communications several times to areas which had been struck by floods and tornados. I won a gold plated Vibroplex speed key during the 1950s in a Morse code receiving contest, at a "Ham Radio" Convention. The contest was conducted in New Orleans by the FCC. My "win" was made possible from my experience as a Press Operator on shipboard during WW2.

My current interests and passion is in maintaining the USS Utah Association web site, and tracing my family history.

Don Johnson: I am the guy that put this book together and am the author of many of the stories. I have published another book using short stories as a basis for the book, titled: "Faith, Family, Friends", which is a faith based Christian inspirational. I served in the Navy from 1969 thru 1992 with a break in service from 1973-1976. I worked my way up the ranks to RM1/E-6 and then was commissioned an Ensign through the Limited Duty Officer program. I am now an Information Technology consultant and most recently promoted to Sales Executive in a small telecommunications/IT systems integration company in Stockton, CA. I am the webmaster for 4 non-profit organizations, the company I work for and my two personal websites—http://www.don-goose.com and http://www.donjohnsonfamily.com. I live in Suisun City, CA and am married to Barbara for 31 years with 3 daughters, 3 granddaughters and 1 grandson, a foster daughter and two foster grandsons. Our foster daughter lost her daughter of 5 months to SIDS this past year.

Larry Matthews: I was a US Navy veteran from 1969 thru 1973. I served aboard USS MAUNA KEA and USS ORISKANY plus shore station duty at Naval Radio Transmitting Facility Dixon, CA. I am the writer of an unpublished novel "American Armageddon", various newspaper articles, and author of more than 17 web pages. I currently reside in Yuba City, California. I am married with 4 teenaged kids and have worked in County Government in California since 1974. 16 years as County Veterans Service Officer and the last 12 as a Child Support Specialist. I worked part time, off and on, as a disc jockey on various radio stations (KAOR, KUBA & COOL 104) from 1967 to 2001. I am presently retired from that profession. My interests are hiking, biking, writing. Like seeing old rock groups in concert (saw Steppenwolf, Paul McCartney, Eric Clapton and Rod Stewart in the past 12 months)and I also enjoy reading and writing about history.

Bob Price: While stationed in Yokosuka, Japan in Nov. '65 I volunteered for duty with an air transportable communication unit (ATCU-100A) which was set up near the airfield in Can-Tho, Vietnam. Team members included Navy radiomen from Hawaii and Japan. The unit was attached to Army Advisory Team 96. Original MK-1 PBR's began arriving at Can-Tho's RAG (River Assault Group) base in May, 1966. Returning to Japan in June, 1966, I finished my tour at the Naval Communications Station, Yokosuka as a second class radioman (RM-2) and reported aboard the USS Annapolis (AGMR-1) for a one year tour in the Tonkin Gulf, arriving just before TET 68'. Married to Suzanne Gallagher in April, 1971, (Divorced in 1996) I have three sons, Rob, Mike and Kevin. Discharged in Feb. 69', I later served in the National Guard as a staff sergeant (E-6) from 1972–1974. Currently, I am a Facility Manager with the U.S. Dept.

of Interior, National Park Service in N.E. Penna. Hobbies include hunting, fishing, photography, reloading and gun collecting. Medals include CAR, NUC, MUC, GCM, NDSM, VSM w/5 stars, VGCM w/palm, VCM w/1960 device, and combat "E" (Annapolis).

Butch Weghorst: I was born 18 Jan 45 in Pasadena, Texas and lived there most of my life. I entered the USN in May of 63 and was separated in March of 68, final discharge was May of 69. I served on the USS Sanctuary (AH-17) from 11/66 to 3/68. Since leaving the service, I have continually worked in the marine electronics industry. I currently work for Furuno USA, Inc. of Camas, WA. I work out of my house and manage a sales territory including the Gulf Coast and inland waterways of the U.S. We sell Radar, depth sounders, GPS, Loran C, various navigation plotters and communications products, both recreational and commercial. I have been with Furuno for over 18 years. I reside in the Houston area known as Clear Lake City, near the NASA Space Center.

Yuvonne Wolf: I was born 20 May 1933 at Callender, Webster Co., Iowa and moved to Brown County, Kansas in 1938. I graduated from Hiawatha, Kansas High School in May 1951, then enlisted in U.S. Navy WAVES on 3 May 1954 at Kansas City, MO., where I attended WAVES Boot Camp at Bainbridge, MD and graduated Boot Camp in July 1954. My duty assignments included: Communications Technician School, Imperial Beach, CA., National Security Agency, Arlington Hall Station, Arlington, VA., Naval Security Station, Washington, D.C., Naval Security Group Activity, Wahiawa, HI, Naval Security Group Headquarters, Washington, D.C., and was honorably discharged from active duty in March 1964. I accepted a position as a civilian employee of the Naval Security Group Headquarters, Washington, D.C. and resigned this position in September 1966 to accept employment in the private sector. I returned in June 1968 as a civilian employee of the Naval Security Group Headquarters, Washington, D.C. I accepted a position in the Registered Publications Department, Naval Security Station, Washington, D.C. In October 1972, the Registered Publications Department became a 4th echelon command under the Naval Security Group Headquarters, Washington, D.C. The Department's title was changed to Director, Communications Security Material System. I later became Head, Policy and Procedures Department for this organization, and retired in June 1988, returning home to Kansas where I continue to enjoy my family and my retirement.

About the Author

Donald Johnson is a retired Navy mustang officer. He began his career after boot camp and radioman school on an oiler that deployed to Vietnam within six months after reporting. He ended his career on an aircraft carrier that became the tip of the sword in Operation Desert Shield. He retired from that aircraft carrier 12 months after returning from the Persian Gulf. He brings to you sea stories, all true, that took place sometime during his career and he has added sea stories, all true, from other sailors and Navy wives who had something they had always wanted to write about and have published. Donald is married to Barbara for over 30 years and has 4 daughters and six grandchildren. He is now a sales executive for a small family owned telecommunications company that provides services to many emergency service organizations (police, fire, ambulance) throughout the Sacramento and San Joaquin valleys

0-595-26102-7